Dante Among the Moderns

Dante's Dream by D. G. Rossetti, courtesy of
Merseyside County Art Galleries, Liverpool, England

DANTE

AMONG THE MODERNS

Edited by Stuart Y. McDougal

The University of North Carolina Press

Chapel Hill and London

Library of Congress Cataloging in Publication Data
Main entry under title:
Dante among the moderns.

1. English literature—20th century—History and
criticism—Addresses, essays, lectures. 2. American
poetry—20th century—History and criticism—Addresses,
essays, lectures. 3. Dante Alighieri, 1265–1321—
Influence—Addresses, essays, lectures. 4. English
literature—Italian influences—Addresses, essays,
lectures. 5. American poetry—Italian influences—
Addresses, essays, lectures. I. McDougal, Stuart Y.
PR473.D27   1985   820'.9'0091   85-4804
ISBN 0-8078-1662-0

Although all of the essays were commissioned for this volume,
the following have appeared in print:

"The Divine Comedy of W. H. Auden" appeared previously in
The Sewanee Review, Vol. 40, Winter 1982.

"Yeats' Romantic Dante" appeared previously in the Special Yeats Issue
of *Colby Library Quarterly*, Vol. 20, No. 2, June 1979.

"Mirroring the Commedia" appeared previously in *Paideuma*, Vol. 10, No. 3, 1981,
and in *Dante in America*, ed. Bartlett Giamatti (Binghamton, 1983).

The editor wishes to thank the American Council of Learned Societies for a
fellowship that enabled him to begin this project, and the Horace H. Rackham
School of Graduate Studies, University of Michigan, for a grant to complete it.

For Nora

CONTENTS

STUART Y. McDOUGAL

Preface

When T. S. Eliot, in a characteristic pronouncement, declared that "Dante and Shakespeare divide the modern world between them,"[1] he could well have added that Dante's impact on the major writers of the modern world had far exceeded that of Shakespeare. Writers as diverse as Arthur Rimbaud, Paul Claudel, Ezra Pound, Giuseppe Ungaretti, Osip Mandelstam, Eugenio Montale, and T. S. Eliot himself have been decisively influenced by this medieval Tuscan poet. The essays in *Dante Among the Moderns* attempt to assess the nature and range of this influence by focusing on Dante's presence in the work of the major British and American modernists, a group that includes W. B. Yeats, Ezra Pound, T. S. Eliot, Samuel Beckett, Wallace Stevens, and W. H. Auden.[2] Dante has dominated the imaginations of these modernists as has no other writer. The striking differences in response to this remote precursor help us to understand the nature of literary influence, clarify the development of each writer, and highlight the multiplicity of literary stances within the modernist movement.

The indebtedness of modern writers to Dante manifests itself in a variety of ways, including citation and allusion, imitation, parody, and the development of a host of Dantean literary strategies, as well as in a continuing dialogue between modernists and Dante. No two writers are influenced by Dante in the same way, but then no two writers have read the same *Commedia*. It is not only the difference between the Dante Yeats encounters in the pages of H. F. Cary's translation and the Dante T. S. Eliot reads in the Temple Classics Edition, with facing Italian and English texts, but also the fact that each modern writer is responding to a precursor who is in large part a creation or projection of his own needs, both poetic and personal. Thus, Yeats places Dante in a tradition of romantic poetry, while Eliot reads Dante as a metaphysical poet. Eliot would have felt no more affinity for Yeats's "romantic Dante," than he would have for Beckett's Dante, or Auden's. As a writer's needs change, so does the nature of Dante's influence on his work. A striking instance of this is Eliot's conversion to the Church of England in 1927, after which he became increasingly concerned with Dante's religious beliefs. Dante, then, is read (and misread) in a variety of ways by the great modernists, and his influence on them is continually changing.

Just as the modernists read different Dantes, so do the essayists in this collection bring their own critical positions to bear on the complex question of literary influence. What is literary influence, and how can it be determined and defined? Implicit in each essay are different answers to these questions, and *Dante Among the Moderns* includes a representative selection of approaches to the subject of literary influence. If, for example, George Bornstein were writing on Ezra Pound, Hugh Kenner on Samuel Beckett, and Glauco Cambon on T. S. Eliot, to cite but three of the essayists, the collection would be a very different one. The diversity of approach indicates the highly problematic nature of literary influence, and hence one of the many difficulties of writing literary history.

Dante's impact on British and American writers has only become important within the last century. As George Bornstein indicates in his essay on Yeats, Dante was rediscovered by the English romantic writers after centuries of relative neglect. The strong interest in Dante which began in the nineteenth century and continues today is an important part of the radical change in literary values which occurred with the romantics and is thus a significant development in modern literary history. The renewed interest in Dante also reveals the need of modern writers for a strong model outside the English literary tradition to help them avoid the often oppressive influence of their own immediate literary precursors, and to enable them to "resuscitate the dead art of poetry," to cite a line (translated from *Purgatorio* 1.7) from Ezra Pound's influential poem, *Mauberley.*

Dante himself had a strong precursor from another literary tradition—Virgil—who exerted a formative influence on his work. John Freccero distinguishes between two different "levels" of influence in the *Commedia*, a poet's use of the materials of a predecessor (in this case, Virgil's *Aeneid*) and his aspiration to poetic or even cultural supremacy, as shown by Dante's relationship to his contemporary, Guido Cavalcanti, as well as his relationship to Virgil. Similar types of influence, Freccero argues, occur between Dante and modern poets, and among modern poets themselves. In short, Freccero finds a model for studying cross-cultural, cross-temporal, and cross-linguistic influence within the *Commedia* itself.

The modern writers represented in this collection do indeed manifest the varieties of influence noted by Freccero and other types as well. Although Dante was a less pervasive influence on the poetry of Yeats than on Pound or Eliot, he was certainly a very important figure in Yeats's development. Yeats adapts Dante's work for at least ten poems, three plays, and a story, and mentions Dante over ninety times in his published prose. George Bornstein chronicles Yeats's uses of Dante as a romantic precursor, and in so doing argues strongly for the continuities between romanticism and modernism. Thus the discovery of Dante by the romantic poets looms large in Bornstein's analysis, and Yeats himself is depicted as a modern romantic poet.

The romantic context is totally absent in Hugh Kenner's essay, since Kenner represents a view of literary history that emphasizes the break between romanticism and modernism, rather than the continuity. Although there is considerable evidence of Dante's presence in Pound's early prose and poetry, Kenner concentrates on *The Cantos*, a work whose scope is "what [has] happened since Dante." Kenner demonstrates how Pound's reading of Dante had shaped his development of the major themes of *The Cantos*. Pound viewed Dante as the inheritor of complex traditions, and Kenner indicates how Dante's example taught Pound to develop and manipulate these and similar traditions in *The Cantos*.

T. S. Eliot, like W. B. Yeats, created a Dante to serve his own needs. But unlike Yeats, Eliot wished to break decisively with his romantic precursors, as well as with his other major poetic precursors in English and American poetry. Eliot created a tradition of metaphysical poetry that had Dante and the poets of the *dolce stil nuovo* as its first and major exemplars, included the English metaphysical poets and the nineteenth century French symbolists, and culminated with Eliot's own work. Dante also suggested to Eliot a model of the poet as exile, who was able to transform the agonies of his personal life into a work of art. Like the relationships between Dante and the other subjects of this collection, Eliot's was an ever changing one, at times poetic, at times personal, and at times religious, although rarely any single one of these alone.

The work of W. H. Auden constitutes a "divine comedy" for Monroe K. Spears, divine because it is concerned with the divinity of the everyday world, and comic because of its use of a strong vernacular speech and because of its happy ending. Spears suggests that Auden's work be divided into three periods which correspond to the three realms of the *Commedia*, an observation that could be made of Eliot's work as well, although Auden's work, unlike Eliot's, is rarely penitential in tone. During Auden's "infernal period" (through 1939), he regarded Dante as an antiquarian figure of limited relevance. An important change occurred for Auden on the eve of the war, as he entered a period of self-reflection and self-examination that Spears calls "purgatorial." Dante provides a model for such activity and becomes a frequent presence in the long poems Auden wrote during the forties. Although the *Purgatorio* remains the primary influence throughout Auden's work, the third stage of Auden's career suggests a parallel with the *Paradiso*. Auden's paradise, however, can be realized on this earth and in this life.

Like Auden's work, Wallace Stevens's poetry is often marked by a "playful use of Dante." Dante is one of Stevens's "inner interlocutors," and it is in "the use of thematic cues" that Stevens's responsiveness to Dante is defined. Glauco Cambon elucidates the analogies between Stevens's work and Dante's and clarifies Stevens's positive attraction to Dante, in spite of his strong opposition to the theology of the *Commedia*. The highly different reactions of, say, Eliot, Auden, and Stevens to this theology are one way of highlighting the range of modernist responses to Dante. In each case the dynamics of influence elucidates different stances within the modernist movement.

Samuel Beckett, who like Auden was from a second generation of modernists, has had a lifelong interest in Dante. As Wallace Fowlie demonstrates, Beckett couples Dante's work in his imagination with that of James Joyce. Beckett's use of Dante follows a pattern observed by John Freccero in Dante's own use of Virgil: "The references move from direct citation . . . to direct translation, to the merest allusion." This pattern characterizes the work of other moderns as well. However, a title like

Dante and the Lobster indicates the nature and extent of Beckett's imaginative transformations. Not even Eliot, one of whose personae imagines himself being "a pair of ragged claws" would dare conjoin the Tuscan master with a crustacean. By the time of such later works as *Waiting for Godot* and *Endgame*, "the example and presence" of Dante has become "more subtle and more significant."

Given the combination of their lifelong fascination with Dante's work and their interest in language and even translation, it is perhaps surprising that none of the great moderns translated Dante, other than as a part of their own work. Ezra Pound spent years translating the poetry of Arnaut Daniel, largely because of Dante's high praise for Daniel, and he devoted even more time to translating the poetry of Dante's contemporary, Guido Cavalcanti. Certainly Dante has been translated frequently in this century; more often in fact, than in any earlier period. Robert Fitzgerald argues that the best of these translations is Laurence Binyon's, done in the shadow of the moderns and with considerable assistance from Ezra Pound. Fitzgerald's essay on Binyon's version is a masterful study of the problems encountered by a twentieth century English translator of medieval Italian, and it demonstrates the extent to which we can call Binyon's translation a modernist work. In supplementing Bornstein's account of nineteenth century translations of Dante and Kenner's essay on Pound, Fitzgerald adds another important chapter to the story of Dante's fortunes in this century and to the literary history of the modernist movement. Fitzgerald's essay forms an appropriate coda to *Dante Among the Moderns*.

NOTES

1. T. S. Eliot, *Dante* (London: Faber and Faber, 1929), p. 51. Reprinted in *Selected Essays* (New York: Harcourt, Brace and Company, 1950), p. 225.

2. The one absent figure is James Joyce, whose relationship to Dante has already been treated in considerable detail by Mary T. Reynolds, *Joyce and Dante: The Shaping Imagination* (Princeton, N.J.: Princeton University Press, 1981) and by Eugene Goodheart, "The Blasphemy of Joycean Art," in *The Failure of Criticism* (Cambridge: Harvard University Press, 1978).

Dante Among the Moderns

JOHN FRECCERO

Virgil, Sweet Father
A Paradigm of Poetic Influence

On the matter of Dante's influence on modern poetry, T. S. Eliot's pronouncements in "Tradition and the Individual Talent" remain more relevant than other more recent theories about what constitutes poetic influence. After seven hundred years, Dante's text, written in a foreign language to begin with, is too remote in history to create the kind of obstacle described by Harold Bloom in his *Anxiety of Influence*—the rival poetic personality with which the younger poet must grapple in order to achieve a poetic identity. The unequalled vastness of the *Divine Comedy* renders the poetic personality even more inaccessible; while almost all modern poets can trace the Dantesque ancestry of some of their verses, none can claim him as a model. To speak of Dante's influence, then, is to speak of the ways in which fragments of a no longer vital tradition have been used, often ironically, in order to shape totally different individual talents. Dante's poetic personality may be safely relegated to the pantheon of tradition, an authority invoked for technical assistance in the accomplishment of thoroughly modern enterprises.

At the same time, the appeal to Dante as literary ancestor in the work of Eliot may be interpreted as a claim to a poetic respectability not possessed by other poets, and especially not by Ezra Pound. Pound sensed in Dante something of the *bien pensant* and the conservative in comparison to the free-thinking daring of Guido Cavalcanti. It is difficult to resist pressing the analogy to apply to Eliot and Pound as well. At this level, the issue of Dante's "influence" may well be a mask for contemporary rivalry: Eliot playing Dante to Pound's Guido, with attendant anxiety, as described by Bloom. To trace one's poetic lineage to Dante is tantamount to claiming the poet's laurels against all other contenders, at least in the case of Eliot.

We may then distinguish two different levels at which it is relevant to speak of "Dantesque influence." There is first of all the fragmentary use of traditional materials in the formation of a new individual talent. At the same time, there is the aspiration to poetic or even cultural supremacy, a contemporary struggle masked by the figure of Dante. It happens that exactly these forms of "influence" were set forth with remarkable clarity in Dante's own text, with the figure of Virgil. On one hand, Dante drew heavily from Virgil, often with ironic intent, reworking themes and images in order to forge a new Christian version of the tradition. He tells us explicitly that Virgil is his master and his *autore*, that it was from him alone that he took the "beautiful style that has done me honor" (Inferno, 1, 87). Other classical authors, notably Ovid, are used in an analogous way, of course, but Virgil's poem provides a structural as well as a verbal model, at least as far as the descent into Hell is concerned. On the other hand, it is the figure of Virgil that is the vehicle for Dante's claim to a certain superiority over Guido Cavalcanti. In a much debated passage of the *Inferno*, Dante seems to suggest, however hesitatingly, that he is privileged to undertake the journey because of his respect for Virgil, whom Guido *perhaps* disdained. That faltering note, in a debated passage, marks the moment in which Dante comes closest to an uncertainty that he nowhere betrays in his relationship to his ostensible model, Virgil. There hovers around the figure of Guido in Dante's work an ambivalence toward the poet whom he once called his "first friend" and whom he helped to send into an exile from which Guido never returned. As the figure of Dante serves Eliot as a vehicle for his rivalry with Pound, so the figure of Virgil serves Dante, in at least one instance in the poem, as a vehicle for his dispute with Guido. By an extraordinary parallel of which Eliot was probably dimly aware, Dante was his precursor not only in poetry, but in his relationship to his contemporaries as well.

There are great differences, of course, between the way that Eliot drew from tradition and the way that Dante used Virgil's text. Whatever the extent to which Eliot's evocations of Dante are deliberately nostalgic or even archeological, there is no doubt that Dante's citations of Virgil are deliberate distortions, at least from the standpoint of modern interpretation. Modern critics are often embarrassed at what seem to be Dante's misunderstandings or even mistranslations of Virgil's text. In Canto 20 of the *Inferno*, for example, Dante puts into the mouth of Virgil an account of the foundation of Mantua that directly contradicts the account of the *Aeneid*. Moreover, the character Virgil urges the pilgrim to discount all other versions he is likely to hear and then compliments him on his exhaustive knowledge of the Roman Epic. Later on, in the *Purgatorio*, the character Statius cites a passage in the *Aeneid*, mistranslating it entirely. Modern translators, in their zeal to protect Dante's reputation as a Latinist, often translate the passage directly from the Latin original, ignoring the Italian (mis-)translation, although Dorothy Sayers is uneasy enough about this that she adds an appendix on the subject to her version of that *cantica*.[1] Dante's apparent mistranslations and the subsequent embarrassment of his translators point up the radical difference between modern and medieval hermeneutics. Even apart from Dante's text, it may be said that the Virgil of antiquity and the Virgil of the Middle Ages differ as archeological reconstruction differs from creative misunderstanding.

One of the reasons that led Dante to choose Virgil as his guide was that Virgil was believed by Christians to have foretold the coming of Christ. This messianic reading of Virgil's *Fourth Eclogue*, referred to by Dante's Statius in the *Purgatorio*, is generally taken as an example of medieval naivete; it might just as well be read as a sophisticated refusal to be guided by "the intentional fallacy." The point is that the text itself, purely apart from Virgil's intended meaning, was believed to have foretold the coming of Christ. This is the meaning of Dante's famous simile comparing Virgil to one who goes by night carrying a lantern behind him, lighting the way for others rather than himself. Rather than a simple container whose contents are to be discovered by the interpreter, the text is the light whereby the *reader is illuminated*.

If we return to the passage concerning Statius with this principle in mind, then it is clear that Virgil's text "meant," not what Virgil intended, but rather what Statius understood. Statius is giving us an account of his conversion, exactly as Augustine does in the eighth book of the *Confessions*. The passage from the *Aeneid* is understood as a moral admonition, not as a text for aesthetic appreciation. It makes no more sense to insist on Virgil's intended meaning in that text than it does to ask what the voices of children really meant when they uttered the words "tolle, lege," that Augustine took as a command to read the Bible and so undergo his conversion. On such a reading of ancient tradition, the author's intention is no better a guide than the character Virgil in the *Purgatorio*, a companion as much in need of enlightenment as the pilgrim himself.

It is with such masterful self-confidence that Dante employs Virgil's text, much as the Middle Ages read the *Fourth Eclogue*, superimposing the Christian revelation on Virgil's own, though thoroughly Roman, typology. Sometimes the distortion is slight, as in the first canto of the poem, where Dante refers to "umile Italia," an obvious reference to Virgil's "low-lying Italy," but then coordinates the words with the phrase "proud Ilium—superbo Ilion," giving to the first words a moral, rather than geographic value. The movement from Troy to Italy is read as a movement from pride ("superbo") to humility ("umile"), adding a dimension in moral allegory to the meaning of the *Aeneid*. On the other hand, the adaptation of the Virgilian underworld amounts to distortion on a vast scale, the realm of the dead transformed into the realm of the damned, destiny transformed into moral choice. The distortion seems to penetrate to every detail, so that, for example, when the poet and his guide cross the river Styx, there is an obligatory echo of the topos of generations of men like fallen leaves—but it is followed, not by the Virgilian amplification referring to migrating birds, but rather to falconry. The souls hurl themselves from the bank "come augel per suo richiamo —like a bird to its lure" (*Inferno* 3.116). A migrating bird must submit to the seasons as humans submit to death. A falcon, on the other hand, has been trained, through a perversion of its natural instinct, to act against its own interests in response to a manipulative intelligence. The change in the simile is tantamount to the difference between the classical Hades and the Christian Hell.

The culmination of Virgilian influence occurs at the point where the character Virgil disappears from the dramatic action. The approach to the Terrestrial Paradise is at the same time Dante's affirmation of his own poetic vocation. It is signaled by angelic voices singing "Manibus o date lilia plenis—Give lilies with full hands" (*Purgatorio* 30.21), which is the only verse of the *Aeneid* (6.883) cited in the original Latin in Dante's text.

Dante uses the phrase to announce the return of Beatrice to Eden, but its sense in Virgil's text is one of definitive loss. In the last verses of the sixth book, in the midst of a prophecy concerning the future glory of Rome, Anchises points out the shade of a prematurely dead youth who might have been a hero, Marcellus. The lilies are symbols of mourning, a funereal gesture, suggesting that death is stronger even than Rome. In the *Purgatorio*, the lilies are of course the lilies of the Resurrection, marking the return of Dante's prematurely dead beloved and the triumph of love over death.

As the pilgrim recognizes the approach of Beatrice, he turns to Virgil for comfort: "Conosco i segni de l'antica fiamma—I recognize the signs of the ancient flame" (*Purgatorio* 30.18). This is a direct translation of Dido's words when she first sees Aeneas: "Agnosco veteris vestigia flammae" (*Aeneid* 4.23). Again, the significance is reversed, for Dido's words express the loss of her husband and dark foreboding of further loss, when she will die on the funeral pyre. The dark Eros is transformed by Dante into trembling of anticipation, once more an affirmation of the power of love over death. Finally, the pilgrim sees that Virgil is gone and calls after him, "Virgilio ... Virgilio ... Virgilio" (*Purgatorio* 30.49–51). Here, perhaps, is an allusion to Virgil's fourth *Georgic* and the moment of Orpheus' loss of Eurydice, the culminating moment of the story of death's triumph over the power of poetry, perhaps the most poignant moment of Virgil's poetry. The borrowed poignancy is allowed to last only an instant, however, for it is interrupted by Beatrice's call to the pilgrim, "Dante," and so marks the moment in the poem when the poet names himself. The failure of Virgil's poetry—a poetry of death, for all of its beauty—is followed by Dante's triumph of life. It is at this point in the poem that Virgil disappears.

The tissue of references to Virgil's text constitutes part of the dramatic action. The references move from direct citation, in the original Latin, to direct translation, to the merest allusion as Virgil fades away. At this point, the character is inseparable from his text and both are supplemented by Dante's poetic coming of age. This farewell to the father—*dolcissimo patre*—is unmarked by the slightest uncertainty.

By contrast, uncertainty and ambiguity abound in the tenth canto of the *Inferno*, where the guidance of Virgil is the central issue and where one of the antagonists is absent from the dispute. While Virgil waits and Dante stands in front of the fiery sepulchers of the heretics, one of them rises to ask, "If you go through this blind prison by high genius, where is my son? Why is he not with you?" Dante recognizes him as Cavalcante, the father of his first friend. He answers, "I do not come on my own. The one who waits over there leads me, perhaps whom your Guido held in disdain—*ebbe a disdegno*." The old man asks neither about Virgil nor about the disdain, but fastens his attention instead on the past tense of the word *ebbe* (held): "How? did you say *held*? Is he no longer alive? Does the sweet light no longer strike his eyes?" Dante hesitates a moment, which Guido's father takes to mean that Guido is dead, whereupon he falls back into the tomb and disappears. In part, the exchange constitutes an anatomy of misunderstanding: the pilgrim assumes that the damned know the present state of affairs and so uses the preterit in order to indicate with the phrase "ebbe a disdegno" a single, isolated action in the past. Cavalcante assumes that the pilgrim knows about the limitations of his knowledge and so, quite naturally, takes the past tense to indicate that his son is dead. The misunderstanding arises from totally conflicting sets of assumptions, the precondition for the sin of heresy portrayed here.

There is more at stake in these lines, however, which becomes apparent when we examine them more closely. It happens that Dante's verses repeat a rhyme scheme that occurs in Guido's most famous poem, *Donna me prega*. The relevant words are italicized in the following citations:

> Le sue parole e 'l mondo de la pena
>   M'avean di constui già letto il *nome*:
>   Però fu la risposta così piena.
> Di subito drizzato gridò: "Come
>   Dicesti. "Elli *ebbe*? Non viv'elli ancora?
>   Non fiere li occhi suoi lo dolce *lome*?"
> Quando s'accorse d'alcuna *dimora*
>   Ch'io facea dinanzi a la risposta
>   Supin riccade, e più non parve fora.   [Inferno 10.64–72]

> In quella parte—dove sta memora
> prende suo stato,—sì formato,—come
> diaffan da *lome*,—d'una scuritate

la qual da Marte—vene, e fa *demora*;
elli è creato—ed ha sensato—*nome*,
d'alma costume—e di cor volontate.

The verses from Guido's poem contain the essence of the theory of love he set forth in his *Canzone*. Love is of the *sensitive* (rather than the intellective) soul; it is a debilitating passion, an obfuscation that proceeds from Mars rather than Venus and its light is essentially darkness. Nothing could be further from Dante's own theory of "enlightenment," represented by Virgil's guidance. The words of Cavalcante echo the words of his son's famous poem, with which Guido manifested the disdain here attributed to him by Dante. Virgil's allegorical dimension of meaning is what Cavalcante is unable to understand in his *cieco carcere* (dark prison), which is the same as saying that he, like his son, is unable to perceive Virgil's light.

Critics have argued about the meaning of "Guido's disdain" ever since the poem began circulating. It is worth noting here that the words are spoken by the *pilgrim*, rather than one of his characters, as is usually the case with passages in the poem that have defied our efforts at interpretation. This suggests that at the heart of the difficulty lies, not some obscure point of doctrine—the situation is clear enough, but rather the uncertainty of Dante himself about which of them, Guido or himself, has the claim to authentic poetic identity: *legitimacy* in their descent from the father. Earlier, in the *Vita Nuova*, there seemed to have been a dispute between them about whose beloved was more beautiful—Giovanna or Beatrice. Dante astonished and scandalized the tradition by referring to Giovanna as "she-who-will-come-first" (*Primavera*, her code name, changed to "Prima verrà"), which is tantamount to suggesting that she was a feminine John the Baptist (Giovanni) to his Beatrice. One could hardly go further in asserting the supremacy of one's own poetry. Here in the *Inferno* it is clear, even if the disdain itself is not, that a similar sort of claim underlies the pilgrim's assertion. Around the edges of that assertion, however, in the hesitancy of the word "forse" (perhaps) and in the halting phrases, remains Dante's lingering doubt.

It may seem absurd to us, given Dante's accomplishment, that his sibling rivalry should focus on a predecessor whose accomplishment was,

from our standpoint, so slight. Yet, as Bloom has noted, in this poetic
version of what Freud called "the family romance," the poetic personality
will often create its own obstacle in the struggle for identity. Guido remains, not only that tormented and somewhat aristocratic sometime
poet, but also Dante's powerful creation of his own first friend and
enemy.

NOTES

1. *The Divine Comedy of Dante Alighieri, Purgatory,* trans. Dorothy Sayers (New York:
Basic Books, n.d.), pp. 343–45.

GEORGE BORNSTEIN

Yeats's Romantic Dante

"When I was fifteen or sixteen my father had told me about Rossetti and Blake and given me their poetry to read; and once at Liverpool on my way to Sligo I had seen *Dante's Dream* in the gallery there, a picture painted when Rossetti had lost his dramatic power and today not very pleasing to me, and its colour, its people, its romantic architecture had blotted all other pictures away," recalled W. B. Yeats in his autobiography.[1] Yeats responded so deeply not to the earlier watercolor at the Tate Gallery but rather to the later oil version of *Dante's Dream at the Time of the Death of Beatrice*, Rossetti's largest picture and one of his most important. Chief among its colors were the red and gold which Yeats thought Shelley had imported from Italy for English poetry; chief among its people were the quester poet and his dead beloved, whom henceforth he might apprehend sometimes in vision but could only join permanently in death; and chief among its elements of "romantic architecture" was a winding stair spiraling upward at the extreme right. One sees how the picture blotted out all others for Yeats. Yet his reminiscence indicates more about his lifelong liaison with Dante than simply the correspondence of painterly details with his own art. Yeats consistently saw Dante as a romantic artist, whether associated with strong early romantics like Blake or with their weaker followers like Rossetti.

If Yeats saw himself as the last romantic, he often saw Dante as the first. The tradition in which Yeats placed himself thus stretched from Dante through Blake and Shelley—the two most important of all poets to him—to his own day. Yeats mentioned Dante over ninety times in his published prose, sometimes at length, and adapted Dante's work for parts of at least ten poems, three plays, and a story. He saw Dante above all as a quest poet with whom he shared devotion to an unattainable woman, political office in a strife-torn land, exile (voluntary in Yeats's case), acceptance of an abstruse system of belief, and a host of poetic goals, not least of which was to become a character in his own work. Yet because Dante belonged to another age, did not dominate English poetic tradition, and never inspired his young Irish admirer to discipleship, Yeats could on occasion elevate him beyond even Blake and Shelley, as a rebellious son will substitute a grandfather for a father in family romance. Although he could criticize Dante too, Yeats more often made him into a foil to the high romantics, a heroic predecessor free from their faults, which were usually those of Yeats at the time, and embodying a near-perfect achievement at which Yeats coincidentally aimed. This happened during two principal periods. In the 1890s Yeats saw Dante as the aesthetic figure of Rossetti's paintings and translations or Blake's illustrations (on which Yeats wrote a long essay), marred only by the tinge of moralism which Blake had detected. But Dante atoned for that by incorporating into his art national and folk elements, just as Yeats diligently sought to ground romanticism in his own native soil. His second period of intense interest in Dante spans the decade from composition in 1915 of *Ego Dominus Tuus*, whose title he found in Rossetti's translation of the *Vita Nuova*, to publication of the first version of *A Vision* in 1925, where Dante appears in Yeats's own phase seventeen. But by then Yeats had grown to prize the dramatic qualities he missed in his 1921 comment on Rossetti's picture. Now Dante emerged as a poet of successful self-dramatization through mask, in contrast to the hapless Keats of *Ego Dominus Tuus*, and of acceptance of dramatic conflict in the world, in contrast to the belabored Shelley of *A Vision*. Yeats not only projected onto Dante his own great mature goal of Unity of Being but also traced the related concepts of antithetical completion and a Vision of Evil back to him. His lifelong sympathetic portrayal resulted in a figure of varied and increasing importance. After exploring the romantic origins of Yeats's interest, this essay analyzes his continual transformations of Dante into a perfected romantic exemplifying his own poetic programs and concludes with his prime poetic adaptations of his predecessor.

Literary history sanctions Yeats's association of Dante with the romantics, for in England the romantics rediscovered Dante after centuries of neglect. That information surprises most modern readers, conditioned directly or indirectly by Eliot's influential description of Dante as "anti-romantic."[2] Yet after Chaucer's overt allegiance, Dante's reputation began a long decline in England and reached a nadir in the early eighteenth century. By 1600, Eliot's admired Donne, for instance, spoke for many of his contemporaries when he "flung away Dant[e] the Italian a man pert enough to bee beloved & to[o] much to bee beeleeved."[3] In contrast, Milton—who became the great precursor of the romantics and perennial bête noire of Eliot—found few sympathizers for his more favorable view of Dante. By the neoclassic period, Chesterfield provided in this as in so much else an accurate register of public taste in citing Dante as an "obscure and difficult" author who "certainly does not think clearly. . . . Though I formerly knew Italian extremely well, I could never understand him; for which reason I had done with him, fully convinced that he was not worth the pains necessary to understand him."[4] Many Augustans shared Chesterfield's censures and found Dante not merely difficult but even crabbed and scholastic. Further, Dante ran roughshod over neoclassic rules and refinements. He seemed bizarre and gothic, capable of occasional power but too often lacking design and decorum. Horace Walpole, for example, lambasted Dante with special fervor as part of a general denunciation of all epic poets but Homer: "Dante was extravagant, absurd, disgusting, in short a Methodist parson in Bedlam."[5] But by the end of the century a countermovement had already set in. If Dante was often rude and unpolished, he could also be sublime and original. The age found its favorite grotesque episode in the story of Ugolino, of which Joshua Reynolds did a famous painting in 1773, and its favorite tender one in the history of Paolo and Francesca. Blake later illustrated these two famous episodes, Shelley helped translate one of them, and they both attracted Yeats.

The romantic period transformed the perverse but pathetic Dante of the Augustans into a powerful visionary fit to rank with Milton and Shakespeare. He acquired immense prestige both for his own achievement and as an antidote to neoclassic norms. The romantics paid repeated tribute to him: one thinks, for example, of Coleridge's 1818 lecture on Dante, Wordsworth's sonnet on Dante's seat in Florence, Byron's *Dante's Prophecy*, Keats's selection of Dante as sole text for a walking tour,

Shelley's *Triumph of Life*, and the aged Blake learning Italian expressly to read Dante. For Yeats, Blake's series of illustrations and Shelley's remarks on Dante in the *Defence* (his favorite critical text) dominated all others. From both he would have learned not just praise but the dynamics of distortion, for Blake's designs embodied intermittent "correction" of Dante's legalism and Shelley's analysis a selective emphasis on Dante as a poet wholly dedicated to love.

As Dante's reputation grew so did the number of his readers, both in the original and in translation. The first full rendering of *The Divine Comedy* into English appeared only in 1802, while Cary's more influential one followed in 1814. Coleridge's praise of Cary's work in his own 1818 lecture touched off an explosion of public interest that sold a thousand copies at once, led to the first of many new editions, and eventually earned Cary a tomb in Westminster Abbey. All the great romantics read Cary's version, as did Yeats after them, and most praised it extravagantly.[6] By 1887 a critic could observe that "from that time forward no man aiming at literary reputation thought his education complete unless he had read Dante in Cary or the original."[7] Young men aiming at such reputation in 1887 included Yeats, who knew no Italian. He read first Cary and then Charles Lancelot Shadwell for the *Comedy* (at least the two parts of it that Shadwell translated) and Dante Gabriel Rossetti for the *Vita Nuova* and lyrics. "I am no Dante scholar, and I but read him in Shadwell or in Dante Rossetti," announced Yeats in 1917.[8] To read those and other nineteenth-century translators was not to read Dante, but to read a Dante filtered through a style and diction derived from romantic practice. The romantics shaped Yeats's view of Dante not only through their influential pronouncements but also through their impact upon a century of translation.

Nineteenth-century self-consciousness about its rediscovery of Dante and an increasing tendency to aestheticize him came together in an essay that Yeats read near the start of his career, Walter Pater's 1892 introduction to Shadwell's *Purgatory*. Here again, as in his better-known pronouncements in *The Renaissance* (which he dedicated to Shadwell) on intensity and the ecstatic moment, Pater anticipates Yeats's early position. He began by citing Voltaire's hostility as reflecting "the general unfitness of the last century in regard to the Middle Age, of whose spirit Dante is the central embodiment."[9] But Pater detected more than a mere taste for medievalism in his own generation's interest. Dante to them articulated the chief concerns of the nineteenth century itself. In particular, Dante displayed the "minuteness" of observation and fine shades of expression necessary to render not merely the external world but, more importantly, the mental phenomena that Pater calls "subjectivities." Ever since Hallam's essay on Tennyson, of course, Victorian critics had found their favorite "subjective" poets in Keats and Shelley, whose impact they rightly saw first on early Tennyson and Browning and then on Rossetti and others. To that tradition Pater tried to graft religious enthusiasm and relevance to "life": "A minute sense of the external world and its beauties, a minute sense of the phenomena of the mind, of what is beautiful and of interest there, a demand for wide and cheering outlooks in religion, for a largeness of spirit in its application to life:—these are the special points of contact between Dante and the genius of our own century." Yeats, like many of his cohorts in the Rhymers' Club of the 1890's, tended to splinter Pater's subjectivity from his social sanctions. For most of the decade Yeats lauded a perceptually sensitive Dante and lamented the religious orthodoxy and engagement with practical life which seemed to stain his subjectivity.

Inspired by Rossetti's painting of Dante's Dream, Yeats early assimilated the Vita Nuova to fin de siècle etiolations of romanticism, but until Pater's essay he thought of the Divine Comedy—when he bothered to think of it at all—as a remote, imposing structure showing by contrast the smallness and yet the subtlety of modern poetry. "Modern writers, the great no less than the small among them, have been heavily handicapped by being born in a lyric age, and thereby compelled for the most part to break up their inspiration into many glints and glimmers, instead of letting it burn in one steady flame," he wrote in obvious recollection of the conclusion to The Renaissance. "It is true that they have their compensations, for the glints and glimmers find their way into many a corner and cranny that never could be reached by the great light of a Divine Comedy or an Iliad."[10] Such thinking led to a hole and corner aestheticism, in which the modern poet refined his sensibility sheltered from the glare of his great predecessors. Yeats could not long hold that stance. Pater revealed to him that Dante, too, ranked with subjective artists, albeit marked by more rigorous religion and more direct involvement with life than the fin de siècle norm. Yeats for the rest of his life would puzzle over the relation between Dante's public system and his personal subjectivity. He at first thought that Dante's vast structures limited imagination and only later came to consider that they liberated it.

Yeats's early and derivative wave of interest in Dante crested in his essays on "William Blake and his Illustrations to the Divine Comedy" (1896) and "William Blake and the Imagination" (1897), now paired in *Ideas of Good and Evil*. Like Yeats's other major statements on Dante, these first ones contrast him with a leading romantic poet. The essay on illustrations treats Blake more sympathetically than Dante, while the later one more typically makes Dante into an ideal romantic poet. The present text of *Ideas of Good and Evil* obscures this chronological progression both by reversing the order of the essays and by dating each of them 1897; in fact, "William Blake and his Illustrations" appeared a year earlier, in *The Savoy* for July, August, and September of 1896. The essay has three parts: an opening section, "His Opinions on Art," explains Blake's admiration for definite outline, minute particulars, and exuberant energy; "His Opinions on Dante" contrasts the systems of the two visionaries; and the final "The Illustrators of Dante" berates Stradanus, Genelli, Schuler, Flaxman, Signorelli, and Gustave Doré ("a noisy and demagogic art"[11]) but praises Botticelli, Giulio Clovio, the little-known Adolph Stürler, and of course Blake. Yeats had known Blake's series of 102 illustrations to the *Comedy* at least since the early nineties, when he had praised that unfinished final work in both his editions of Blake.[12]

The essay interpreted both Blake and Dante as ancestors of nineteenth-century aesthetes. Yeats sounds like Hallam in arguing that Blake "strove to embody more subtle raptures, more elaborate intuitions than any before him," and he imitates Pater in valuing " 'the minute particulars of life,' the little fragments of space and time, which are flooded by beautiful emotion" (E&I, 127, 135). The phrases describe not the frenzied Blake of Yeats's maturity, who beat upon the wall till truth obeyed his call, but a Blake seen through the spectacles of late Victorian subjectivity. Yeats consigned Dante to the same camp. He disparaged those who would distinguish Blake's world from Dante's, "as if Dante's world were more than a mass of symbols of colour and form and sound which put on humanity, when they arouse some mind to an intense and romantic life that is not theirs" (E&I, 141). This view reduces Dante to a source of exquisite sensory stimulation that the spectator can anthropomorphize, as Yeats liked to do in the manner of Rossetti. It also reduces the possible poetic adaptation of Dante to local effects.

Eager to preserve Dante's subjectivity, Yeats rejected his broader system under guise of comparing it to Blake's. He fleshed out Blake's scattered comments on Dante into a diabolical reading of the Italian parallel to Blake's own transformation of Milton. "Dante saw devils where I saw none," said Blake. "I see good only" (E&I, 131). In Yeats's sympathetic elaboration, Dante emerged as a great poet contaminated by a philosophy of judgment and punishment which secretly derived from the absorption in worldly affairs which it sought to condemn; Dante had mistaken Satan, the true architect of his Hell, for his divinity, and in symbolizing God by the Primum Mobile he chose the symbol farthest removed from the human form divine. This diabolical reading held that "Dante, who deified law, selected its antagonist, passion, as the most important of sins," but that "Blake, who deified imaginative freedom, held 'corporeal reason' for the most accursed of things" (E&I, 139). Against this it is futile to argue that Dante, as a Christian, neither deifies law nor makes passion the most important sin (indeed, in both *Inferno* and *Purgatorio* passion is the least severe sin), for Yeats does not really mean to criticize Dante. He means to convince himself that his own preoccupation with abstract system menaces his creative life as poet. He in fact shared Dante's belief in a spiritual order existing independently of man, and his salvation as artist came when he learned to use that order to free rather than fetter his own imagination.

If Yeats's essay did not advance the state of Dante scholarship, it did contribute to Dante studies in a way which unfortunately backfired upon the controversial *Savoy*. The only Blakean illustrations to the *Comedy* already available were the seven plates he had managed to engrave before his death. Along with two of those engravings—*The Circle of Thieves* and Yeats's favorite, *Paolo and Francesca*, which he wanted to use as frontispiece for *Ideas of Good and Evil*—the *Savoy* printed for the first time eight of Blake's other designs as accompaniment to the essay.[13] The reproductions both disseminated these important illustrations to an influential audience and led to the failure of the magazine. W. H. Smith and Son, the booksellers who controlled the railway stalls, objected to the frankness of the designs and refused henceforth to carry the *Savoy*. As Yeats tells the story, Smith's manager objected particularly to Blake's version of *Antaeus Setting*

Virgil and Dante upon the Verge of Cocytus, which he apparently mistook for a Beardsley drawing and feared would offend young ladies (A, 323). Symons as editor lamented this philistinism in his farewell to his readers.[14] To Yeats the episode provided another sad example of the conflict between elite art and a mass audience.

Blake did not long have the best of Dante in Yeats's prose. Yeats had made a pass at impartiality even in the essay on illustrations to the *Comedy*. Although clearly sympathetic to the diabolical reading, he claimed to have taken Blake's side simply because Dante enjoyed so much greater public knowledge. "By thus contrasting Blake and Dante by the light of Blake's paradoxical wisdom, and as though there was no important truth hung from Dante's beam of the balance, I but seek to interpret a little-understood philosophy rather than one incorporate in the thought and habits of Christendom," he insisted ingenuously (E&I, 134). The next year Yeats redressed the balance in his second and shorter Blake essay. The truth that weighed heaviest from Dante's beam turned out to be the very use of material incorporate in the thought and habits of Christendom noted a year earlier. Towards the end of his short "William Blake and the Imagination" (1897) Yeats invoked Dante to explain Blake's continuing inaccessibility:

> [Blake] spoke confusedly and obscurely because he spoke of things for whose speaking he could find no models in the world about him. He was a symbolist who had to invent his symbols; and his counties of England, with their correspondence to tribes of Israel, and his mountains and rivers, with their correspondence to parts of a man's body, are arbitrary.... He was a man crying out for a mythology, and trying to make one because he could not find one to his hand. Had he been a Catholic of Dante's time he would have been well content with Mary and the angels; or had he been a scholar of our time he would have taken his symbols ... from Norse mythology; or ... Welsh mythology ... or have gone to Ireland and chosen for his symbols the sacred mountains, along whose sides the peasant still sees enchanted fires, and the divinities which have not faded from the belief ... and have been less obscure because a traditional mythology stood on the threshold of his meaning. [E&I, 114]

Through the example of Blake, that passage analyzes a major obstacle for modern poets more acutely than it proposes a remedy. Although Blake's symbolism owes more to tradition than Yeats allowed, he not only invented his own myth but thought that he had to in order to avoid enslavement by another man's. Yet avoiding enslavement also meant avoiding easy accessibility. So did construction of the myths of most modern poets. Pound's correlation of disparate traditions, Eliot's adaptation of Indian, Christian, and Middle Eastern fertility rites in *The Waste Land*, or even Stevens's attempt to evolve a supreme fiction all rank with Blake's mythopoetic achievement but similarly lack the ready comprehension that Dante's adaptation of Catholic myth bore for readers of his time. Yeats sought to ground his own work in Irish soil and continually claimed to have corrected romanticism by fastening it to national mythology. "I could not endure, however, an international art, picking stories and symbols where it pleased," he wrote of himself at the time of *Oisin*. "Might I not . . . create some new *Prometheus Unbound*; Patrick or Columcille, Oisin or Finn, in Prometheus' stead; and, instead of Caucasus, Cro-Patrick or Ben Bulben? Have not all races had their first unity from a mythology that marries them to rock and hill?" (*A*, 194). But Yeats's proposed remedy works only a little better than the cosmopolitanism he detested. Even in his own time his use of Irish material caused problems even among Irish readers, most of whom learned about Oisin or Finn from recent books rather than from ongoing tradition. And Blake would not have been more accessible had he taken his symbols from Norse, Welsh, or Irish tradition. They would have caused his non-Norse readers, say, as much trouble as Yeats's Celticism has made for his non-Irish ones. Our time offers no counterpart to Dante's advantages.

Yeats's drive to anchor romanticism in Irish tradition led to his early insistence that Dante drew his Christian materials partly from folklore. His favorite example came from *Inferno* 13, whose souls imprisoned in trees he likened to native Celtic myth.[15] In a burst of assimilative enthusiasm he described Dante, along with Homer, Aeschylus, Sophocles, Shakespeare, Goethe, and Keats as "folklorists with musical tongues" and insisted that Dante exploited folk sources "continuously." Yeats offers such parallels and claims more as literary propaganda than as scholarly proof, and in utilizing his own native folklore he usually does not mean to imitate Dante. Rather, he invokes Dante as sanction for his own enterprise. For Yeats, folklore implied not just ready-made audience but contact with vital imaginative tradition which had survived the onslaughts of European science and mechanism. "Europe belongs to Dante and the witches' sabbath, not to Newton," he affirmed later (Lett, 807).

Dante had little direct impact on Yeats's early verse, but the one clear adaptation, the much-revised The Countess Cathleen in Paradise, follows the precept of grounding broader vision in local lore. Even the final title shows that, for Cathleen belongs to Irish legend but the vision of Paradise to Dante. The original (1891) version of the poem sounded more like Rossetti than Dante, offering Cathleen as Blessed Damozel in its last quatrain:

> She goes down the floor of Heaven,
> Shining bright as a new lance;
> And her guides are angels seven,
> While young stars about her dance.[16]

Yeats brought the lines closer to Dante in his 1895 revision:

> With white feet of angels seven,
> Her white feet go glimmering,
> And above the deep of heaven,
> Flame on flame and wing on wing.

The vision of white angels with flame and wings in Paradise derives from Paradiso 31:

> Faces had they of flame, and wings of gold:
> The rest was whiter than the driven snow;
> And, as they flitted down into the flower . . .   [Cary, 514]

Yeats indicated his Dantesque source in a 1927 letter, where he discussed first the flames of purgatory and then Beatrice before quoting the final version of the poem—in which he likened Cathleen to a dancer—and then asking, "is there jealousy in such dancers or did Dante find them as little so as colour is of colour?" (Lett, 731–32). Cathleen thus becomes a surrogate Beatrice, entering into the angelic company of the paradisal rose. The early context of the song in the play The Countess Cathleen supports the association, for after singing the lyric the First Spirit explains that he and his company must return to the "rose by the seat of God, /

Which is among the angelic multitude,"[17] just as Dante's canto opens by describing the rose in which the spirits abide: "In fashion, as a snow white rose, lay then / Before my view the saintly multitude." Yeats, of course, had early known Dante's rose of the *Paradiso*, but except for this one lyric it seems not to have affected his own Rose poems. Besides gaelicizing Dante and following Pater's appreciation of his subtle detail, the poem evinces Blake's "correction" of Dante's legalism, for the Countess enters paradise instead of an inferno because she has sold her soul to the devils out of love for her starving dependents.

Brooding upon the hostile reception to *The Countess Cathleen* led Yeats to his most habitual use of Dante during the decade and a half from 1900 to 1914. Hostile nationalist critics had attacked the *Countess* and other plays for tarnishing the image of Ireland; an Irishwoman would not, like Cathleen, sell her soul to the devil. Dante offered a means of riposte against demands for a cardboard virtue. "The greater portion of the *Divine Comedy* is a catalogue for the sins of Italy," wrote Yeats in *Samhain* for 1905.[18] Imbued with Shelley's *Defence*, Yeats thought that a poet could best shape his country by refusing passing partisanship and instead developing national imagination. Dante had done that. "A nation can only be created in the deepest thought of its deepest minds. . . . They create national character," he wrote in 1910. "Goethe, Shakespeare, Dante, Homer have so created."[19] Yeats, like Joyce, similarly wanted to forge the uncreated conscience of his race. It was a romantic goal, and for the modern poet meant alienation from his society. A year before describing the *Comedy* as a catalogue of Italian vice Yeats argued that "there never have been men more unlike any Englishman's idea of himself than Keats or Shelley. . . . We call certain minds creative because they are among the moulders of their nation and are not made upon its mould" (E, 158).

As he remade his mind and art during this period, Yeats more and more came to value the interrelation of disparate emotions through a consistent system of imagery. The molder of a nation had to organize its psyche. He again paired Dante with a romantic writer to illustrate his discovery:

All art is sensuous, but when a man puts only his contemplative nature and his more vague desires into his art, the sensuous images through which it speaks become broken, fleeting, uncertain, or are chosen for their distance from general experience, and all grows unsubstantial and fantastic. . . . If we are to sojourn there that world must grow consistent with itself, emotion must be related to emotion by a system of ordered images, as in the *Divine Comedy*. . . . Shelley seemed to Matthew Arnold to beat his ineffectual wings in the void, and I only made my pleasure in him contented pleasure by massing in my imagination his recurring images of towers and rivers, and caves with fountains in them, and that one Star of his, till his world had grown solid underfoot and consistent enough for the soul's habitation. [E&I, 293–94]

The passage reveals more than mere progress beyond an earlier conception of Dante's work as a congeries of aesthetic moments to a new appreciation of its architectonic precision. Like much of Yeats's criticism, it masks an astute self-evaluation under guise of considering poets to whom he felt akin. The opening description of an unsubstantial or fantastic world resulting from fleeting images based only on the poet's contemplative nature and vaguer desires fits Yeats's mature conception of his own early work. Although he had tried to deploy symbols like the rose and cross, and although a scholar as erudite as Allen R. Grossman can discern a systematic structure in the early work,[20] most readers find a deficiency like that described above. More importantly, Yeats needed to find it. He needed later to distort that early work through heightening its defects, as he needed to distort the precursors who inspired it, to free himself to create his own mature achievement. The pairing here of Dante and Shelley both joins two poets whom Yeats could use as models and implies why he became increasingly hostile to Shelley but receptive to Dante. For just as Yeats had written earlier "in imitation of Shelley" (A, 66), so does he stand closer to him in his manner of interrelating images. Dante had constructed his imaginative system out of traditional Christianity, but Shelley had massed his towers, rivers, caves, and stars from more eclectic sources. So, too, did Yeats garner the recurrent symbols of his mature phase—which he once identified as sun, moon, tower, mask, tree, and bird[21]—and he could find a benevolent (because more distant) sanction in Dante while he saw a threatening (because closer) similarity in Shelley.

Fascination with the most important image for a poet's own character, the mask, powered Yeats's resurgence of interest in Dante for the decade from 1915 to 1925. One of the most complete early formulations, *Ego Dominus Tuus*, makes Dante a paradigm of the poet successfully creating an appropriate mask. The title itself comes from the first commandment by way of the *Vita Nuova*, which Yeats cites in Rossetti's translation at the start of his gloss on the poem in *Per Amica Silentia Lunae* (M, 326). Early in the *Vita Nuova* Love comes to Dante's chamber in a dream vision during which He speaks many things, of which "ego dominus tuus" becomes one of the few Dante can understand and the only one he records. Thomas Vance has shrewdly surmised the importance of the passage: "Dante's fatal commitment of his life to the love of Beatrice is identical with his initiation as a poet,"[22] for after this scene follows the first sonnet. But the application to Yeats lies not in the parallel, as Vance supposes, but in the contrast. For Dante's Love, as desire for the earthly Beatrice that becomes *caritas* for the heavenly Beatrice, Yeats substitutes the poet's passion for his antiself. Yeats's commitment not to his old love for Maud Gonne but to his new dialectic between artist and work initiates the new phase of his poetic career.

The poem itself centers on the contrast between Dante and Keats, from which Dante again emerges as perfected romantic. Ille corrects Hic's naive notion by arguing that Dante created in his poetry an image of an antiself opposite to his ordinary personality:

Hic.   And yet
The chief imagination of Christendom,
Dante Alighieri, so utterly found himself
That he has made that hollow face of his
More plain to the mind's eye than any face
But that of Christ.
Ille.   And did he find himself
Or was the hunger that had made it hollow
A hunger for the apple on the bough
Most out of reach? and is that spectral image
The man that Lapo and that Guido knew?
I think he fashioned from his opposite
An image that might have been a stony face
Staring upon a Bedouin's horse-hair roof

From doored and windowed cliff, or half upturned
Among the coarse grass and the camel-dung.
He set his chisel to the hardest stone.
Being mocked by Guido for his lecherous life,
Derided and deriding, driven out
To climb that stair and eat that bitter bread,
He found the unpersuadable justice, he found
The most exalted lady loved by a man.

In contrast, Keats created not an antiself but simply a satisfied heightening of his normal character:

Hic.   And yet
No one denies to Keats love of the world;
Remember his deliberate happiness.
Ille.   His art is happy, but who knows his mind?
I see a schoolboy when I think of him,
With face and nose pressed to a sweet-shop window,
For certainly he sank into his grave
His senses and heart unsatisfied,
And made—being poor, ailing and ignorant,
Shut out from all the luxury of the world,
The coarse-bred son of a livery-stable keeper—
Luxuriant song.   [VP, 368–70]

   This ascribes to Dante and Keats the same drive—a hunger for things of the world, represented by Dante's lechery and Keats's more generalized luxury. The difference lies in the resultant work. While Keats's luxuriant song became a substitute for the satisfactions denied him by life, Dante's severe ecstasy became antithetical to the worldly satisfaction he craved: his work incorporated the dialectic between his hollow and human selves. "All happy art seems to me that hollow image, but when its lineaments express also the poverty or the exasperation that set its maker to the work, we call it tragic art," explained Yeats. "Keats but gave us his dream of luxury; but while reading Dante, we never long escape the conflict . . ." (M, 329). This interpretation catches Keats's desire for sensuous fulfillment but misses his crucial insistence upon the obliteration of ego through negative capability. It works a little better for Dante, about whom we have less biographical information, though Yeats stands on safer ground in the prose account when he yokes lust to political anger as twin motives. But the interpretation works best of all for Yeats himself, who has again performed a self-examination under cover of literary criticism. The description of Keats closely fits Yeats's own art of the nineties, that luxuriant song produced by a poet perpetually nervous about his ancestry and education, and the portrait of Dante limns the kind of poet Yeats wanted to become (and who found in Dante "my own mood between spiritual excitement, and the sexual torture" [Lett 731]). Indeed, the contrast between Keats and Dante opens by opposing "the gentle, sensitive mind" of modern aesthetes to the sterner "nonchalance of the hand" Yeats wanted to recover from past artists.

Yeats culled the information for his portrait mostly from readily accessible literary sources, principally Dante's own work,[23] but commentators have erred in ascribing his image of Dante in exile ("To climb that stair and eat that bitter bread") directly to Cacciaguida's famous description in Paradiso 17:

> Thou shalt prove
> How salt the savour is of other's bread;
> How hard the passage, to descend and climb
> By other's stairs.   [Cary, 446]

Yeats's lines ultimately derive from Dante's, of course, but they do so by way of Rossetti's paraphrase in his poem Dante at Verona. Rossetti used Cacciaguida's remarks as epigraph but transformed them into Yeats's diction in two freer renderings during the poem itself:

> Of the steep stairs and bitter bread   [line 22]

and

> that bitter bread; / And . . . those stairs   [lines 501–2]

Yeats clearly remembered Rossetti in attaching "bitter" to "bread" and the demonstrative adjective (though plural instead of singular) to "stairs." Rossetti's poem itself dramatized the role of Dante that most fascinated Yeats, the visionary poet in exile.

Dante's life showed the penchant for solitude that Yeats ascribed to all subjective artists. Exile had forced Dante into gregarious circumstances which Yeats as public man knew well. They sprang from both poverty and politics. Just as Dante had needed to please princes and courtiers, so did Yeats contend first with the Abbey company and audiences and then with the duties of a senator and Nobel Prize winner. In 1919 and again in 1925 he cited sympathetically Dante's autobiographical remarks in the first treatise of the *Convito*: "Dante in that passage in the *Convito* which is, I think, the first passage of poignant autobiography in literary history . . . in describing his poverty and his exile counts as his chief misfortune that he has had to show himself to all Italy and so publish his human frailties that men who honoured him unknown honour him no more. Lacking means, he lacked seclusion, and he explains that men such as he should have but few and intimate friends."[24]

By 1925 the *Convito* seemed properly not the first "poignant" but the first "modern" autobiography. It presented the earliest self-conscious artist of the modern gyre, whose psyche operated in terms of the dialectic of will and antithetical mask; by impressing that dialectic upon an abstract system, he achieved in the *Divine Comedy* the first modern victory of personality. Such a poet found his artistic mask in the passionate quester who stood apart from society. As man he sought to retire from partisan rancor to philosophic solitude. Yeats particularly approved Dante's refusal of a tainted Florentine pardon in the Ninth Epistle, from which he twice quoted to his own correspondents: "Cannot I anywhere look upon the stars and think the sweet thoughts of philosophy?" (*Lett*, 849, 882).

Yeats's own sweet thoughts of philosophy matured into *A Vision*, which contains the last of his major discussions contrasting Dante to a romantic. The entire work has a Dantesque side. In translating the *Comedy* Cary had chosen *The Vision* as title, with *Hell, Purgatory, and Paradise of Dante Alighieri* as subtitle. More importantly, Yeats structured his work around an abstract system almost as geometric as Dante's, and he, too, selected historical personages to exemplify its classifications. He hoped that his esoteric system would free his imagination as he thought that medieval Christianity had freed Dante's. "I wished for a system of thought that would leave my imagination free to create as it chose and yet make all that it created, or could create, part of the one history, and that the soul's," he wrote in his original dedication. "The Greeks certainly had such a system, and Dante—though Boccaccio thought him a bitter partisan and therefore a modern abstract man—and I think no man since"

(1925V, xi). Most important of all, Yeats ascribed the highest goal of his system—the Unity of Being resulting from the antithetical mask's capacity to unite us to our true selves—to Dante: "the self so sought is that Unity of Being compared by Dante in the Convito to that of 'a perfectly proportioned human body'" (V, 82). As scholars have realized despite Yeats's persistent assertions,[25] Dante does not make such a comparison there. Why Yeats should thus repeatedly err in citing a source for one of his principal doctrines remains a mystery, but I should like to suggest that he may have faultily remembered two passages from the Third Treatise, which in an 1887 translation ran: "Man is the most wonderful, considering how in one form the Divine Power joined three natures; and in such a form how subtly harmonized his body must be. It is organized for all his distinct powers; wherefore, because of the great concord there must be, among so many organs, to secure their perfect response to each other" and "the beauty of the body is the result of its members in proportion as they are fitly ordered. . . ."[26] Yeats's phantom translation accords well with both those passages and the general tenor of the Convito, and his mistaken lineage for his cherished concept signifies less than does his obvious desire to claim a Dantesque ancestry for it.

The habit of contrasting Dante with a romantic poet as alternate self-images culminated in the crucial formulation of phase seventeen in A Vision, the same phase to which Yeats privately assigned himself. The 1925 text used Dante and Shelley as sole examples (the brief paragraph on Landor was added for the 1937 revision). Yeats calls the man of this phase Daimonic because he can most easily attain Unity of Being. The Daimonic man does that by finding a true mask of simplification through intensity, which allows his creative imagination to forge an Image of desire in defiance of the inevitable loss which constitutes his fate. As Yeats explains, "This Mask may represent intellectual or sexual passion; seem some Ahasuerus or Athanase; be the gaunt Dante of the Divine Comedy; its corresponding Image may be Shelley's Venus Urania, Dante's Beatrice, or even the Great Yellow Rose of the Paradiso" (V, 141). This illuminates a genuine if obvious affinity between Dante and Shelley, who admired him; the corresponding mask for Yeats would be the lover in his early verse and the towered philosopher of his later work. But the investigation goes increasingly awry in contrasting the relation between the life and art of the two poets. Yeats lambastes Shelley for inability to "see anything that opposes him as it really is": Shelley's millenarian hopes for the future of mankind constituted a false image for the mask and thus led him into caricatures of evil, mental instability, vague and cloudy art, and automatonism rather than poetic invention. I have argued elsewhere that these strictures so clash with both the sceptical Shelley and with Yeats's earlier and more accurate views on him that they become intelligible only as an attempt to throw off the poet who had "shaped my life"[27] and to emerge into artistic independence. The critique fits Yeats's own work of the 1890s better than it does Shelley's. Correspondingly, the portrait of Dante, while more accurate historically, offers principally a self-image of Yeats as he wished to become:

> Dante, who lamented his exile as of all possible things the worst for such as he, and sighed for his lost solitude, and yet could never keep from politics, was, according to a contemporary, such a partisan, that if a child, or a woman, spoke against his party he would pelt this child or woman with stones. Yet Dante, having attained, as poet, to Unity of Being, as poet saw all things set in order, had an intellect that served the *Mask* alone, that compelled even those things that opposed it to serve, and was content to see both good and evil. . . . Dante suffering injustice and the loss of Beatrice, found divine justice and the heavenly Beatrice, but the justice of *Prometheus Unbound* is a vague propagandist emotion and the women that await its coming are but clouds. [V, 143–44]

While truer to its overt subject than the remarks on Shelley, this account epitomizes the poetic goals of the mature Yeats. He longed for a Unity of Being to render both good and evil convincingly rather than to produce the vague emotion and cloudy women he had grown to suspect in his early work. We have only to remember incidents like Dante's pleasure in Filippo Argenti's suffering in *Inferno* 8 or his abuse of Bocca degli Abbati in *Inferno* 32 to see that Yeats subtly distorts Dante's view of evil. Not only does the entire *Comedy* share a structure which condemns evil, but the *Inferno* shows in detail the replacement of Dante's initial tears and sympathy for the inmates of Hell by a sterner moralism. Yeats overstates his case in developing his true contention that Dante's view of both good and evil carries conviction. Yeats's phrase "content to see" applies better to the mature work he was then writing or would write, to *The Gyres* for example, in which acceptance on occasion degenerates into indifference or acquiescence.

Often Yeats used the notion of a Vision of Evil to compare Dante with other writers. He capitalized the phrase in *A Vision* and elsewhere to indicate that he meant not a mere vision of evil but rather a vision of both good and evil informing "the world as a continual conflict" (*V*, 144). Need to divorce himself from his chief precursors led to continual misperception that the romantics, like Shelley, lacked such a quality. But two writers to whom he also liked to compare Dante had it—Villon and Balzac. By accurately perceiving evil, both enabled themselves to detect an actual rather than imaginary good as well. They avoided the pitfalls of false optimism. "Had not Dante and Villon understood that their fate wrecked what life could not rebuild, had they lacked their Vision of Evil, had they cherished any species of false optimism, they could but have found a false beauty," concluded Yeats (*A*, 273[28]). So, too, would have Balzac, "the only modern mind which has made a synthesis comparable to that of Dante" (*E*, 269). The *Comédie humaine* had closed a counter-movement to the *Divine Comedy* (*E&I*, 468), and Yeats saw his own work as heralding a return to Europe "upon its knees" before the supernatural. The Vision of Evil became a sort of litmus paper for determining whether a writer had achieved Unity of Being in his work. Poets like Dante or Shakespeare "sought no impossible perfection" either in the world or in their lives but only in their own artifice (*M*, 333). The intellect of man was forced to choose.

Yeats's increasingly unfavorable comparisons of the romantics to Dante do not imply the same attitude as do those of T. S. Eliot. Writing often from a militant antiromanticism, Eliot discerned in Dante the order, morality, and maturity that he thought romantics would forever lack. In contrast, Yeats generally wrote from a proromantic position and saw Dante as a sort of perfected romantic realizing the romantics' goals while avoiding their supposed failures in execution. Portions of his literary criticism became a disguised psychomachia, with Dante as exemplar of what Yeats wanted to become and the romantics of what he feared he had been. The resultant poetry owes less to Dante than does that of Eliot or Pound, whose debt the two following essays demonstrate. Although Dante functions chiefly in Yeats's critical speculations, he did affect some of the creative work, as we have already seen. Rather than rehearse the parallels,[29] I should like instead to focus on the two most important cases, *The Second Coming* and *Byzantium*, to show Yeats's difference from Dante before concluding with analysis of his one sustained effort at modern Dantesque composition, *Cuchulain Comforted*.

The Second Coming (VP, 401) projects into poetry the prose penchant for linking Dante with the romantics. Its principal literary allusions systematically reverse their sources. Just as the famous lines "The best lack all conviction, while the worst / Are full of passionate intensity" counter the Last Fury's speech in Act One of *Prometheus Unbound* and the phrase "stony sleep" plays against Blake's usage in *The Book of Urizen*, so do the opening lines

> Turning and turning in the widening gyre
> The falcon cannot hear the falconer

both echo and revise the description of Geryon at the end of *Inferno* 17:

> As falcon, that hath long been on the wing,
> But lure nor bird hath seen, while in despair
> The falconer cries, "Ah me! thou stoop'st to earth,"
> Wearied descends, whence nimbly he arose
> In many an airy wheel, and lighting sits
> At distance from his lord in angry mood . . .   [Cary, 88–89]

Not only does Geryon's flight trace a gyre, but his human head and animal body recall the shape of Yeats's rough beast. The simile of a falcon refusing the command of his master particularly suits an image of fraud like Geryon, who shuttles between the circle of the violent and the *malebolge* of the fraudulent and malicious. Yeats carries over these associations into a view of history which radically opposes Dante's own. *The Second Coming* suggests the Christian scheme of history even in its title. Yet it replaces the meaningful and finite span of that history with an endless and meaningless succession of cycles: the "second" coming could just as well be the "nth," and is in fact the third implied by the poem. The wit of Yeats's allusion lies in using a metaphor from one of the great Christian achievements of order to describe a disorder inaugurating a new historical phase which will reverse that of Christian civilization itself. Christianity is a truth for Dante but a source of metaphors for Yeats.[30]

The use of Dantesque devices which reveal Yeats's distance from his predecessor recurs in *Byzantium*. Not only does the speaker's uncertainty about whether he confronts "an image, man or shade" recall Dante's confusion about whether Virgil be "shade, or certain man" in *Inferno* 1, but in earlier drafts the mummy functioned as a Virgil-like guide to the speaker.[31] The flames constitute the chief Dantesque echo in the final version. They recall in several ways the flames and fire of *Purgatory* 25–27, whose presence burns even clearer in the prose sketch:

> tall flames wind and unwind
> And in the flames dance spirits, by that their agony made pure
> And though they are all folded up in flame
> It cannot singe a sleeve.

Rather than unravel the details in sources, I mean instead to emphasize two distinctions between Yeats's polysemous symbolism and that of Dante. First, except for the "texts for exposition" of *A Vision*, Yeats's practice seldom depends for interpretation on a preexistent and homogenous body of doctrine that he can count on readers knowing or on a symbolic sense (as opposed to the particular meaning) that he can count on them to expect. As Dante explains in the letter to Can Grande, or in the opening of the *Convito*, his work follows the four recognized senses of medieval literature, usually referred to as the literal and the three general allegorical senses of tropological (pertaining to the individual), anagogical (pertaining to the afterlife), and formally allegorical (pertaining to Christ or the Church). Dante illustrates these by the famous example of the exodus from Egypt, but we could just as easily use the fires of his own Purgatory, which at once literally burn, tropologically show the purification of the soul from lust, anagogically the progression from body to spirit in the afterlife, and allegorically the redemption through Christ. No such scheme fits Yeats's symbolism. He draws from diverse and often philosophically contradictory sources and elaborates his meaning in senses developed by the poem itself rather than standing apart from it. Thus, the fires of *Byzantium* pertain at least both to purification after death and to artistic creativity, but the poem itself must define those senses rather than operate in terms of the reader's inherent expectation of them. Second, elevation of artistic process itself as a primary subject for the symbolism divides this poem from Dante. Dante, of course, often refers to his art and its difficulties, but concentration on creative aesthetic process as both subject and figurative sense seems a distinctively post-romantic phenomenon, which Yeats shares with many other modern poets.

Deepening steadily throughout his literary career, Yeats's fascination with Dante culminated in a poem finished just two weeks before his death, *Cuchulain Comforted*. In frankly adapting Dante to the needs of a contemporary poet, that lyric forms a fit analogue to the stunning utilizations of Dante in the last major poem by Yeats's idol Shelley, *The Triumph of Life*, and by his rival Eliot, *Little Gidding*. Here is Yeats:

> A man that had six mortal wounds, a man
> Violent and famous, strode among the dead;
> Eyes stared out of the branches and were gone.
>
> Then certain Shrouds that muttered head to head
> Came and were gone. He leant upon a tree
> As though to meditate on wounds and blood.
>
> A Shroud that seemed to have authority
> Among those bird-like things came, and let fall
> A bundle of linen. Shrouds by two and three
>
> Came creeping up because the man was still.
> And thereupon that linen-carrier said:
> "Your life can grow much sweeter if you will
>
> "Obey our ancient rule and make a shroud;
> Mainly because of what we only know
> The rattle of those arms makes us afraid.
>
> "We thread the needles' eyes, and all we do
> All must together do." That done, the man
> Took up the nearest and began to sew.
>
> "Now must we sing and sing the best we can,
> But first you must be told our character:
> Convicted cowards all, by kindred slain,
>
> "Or driven from home and left to die in fear."
> They sang, but had nor human tunes nor words,

Though all was done in common as before;

They had changed their throats and had the throats of birds.

[VP, 634–35]

This recalls Dante not only in its terza rima but also in its subject and setting, the fate of a famous personage in the afterlife. Its twenty-five lines seem a portion of a canto from the Comedy. The resemblance extends even to particulars. F. A. C. Wilson has suggested the appropriate similarity of this setting to the Valley of Negligent Rulers in Purgatory 7–8, while T. R. Henn first noticed the parallel between Yeats's shades, who "thread the needles' eyes," and those of the sodomites who gaze "As an old tailor at his needle's eye" (Cary, 74) in Inferno 15.[32]

Even in this most Dantesque of his poems Yeats shows a distance. The tailor image, in Dante's poem a sign of the impaired perception of the squinting sodomites in contrast to the clearer sight of Virgil and Dante, becomes in Yeats's a neutral or even positive activity of the cowards, which Cuchulain must imitate. The poem itself defines the range of application of its symbolism, with a slight assist from the eschatology of A Vision (Cuchulain appears to be in the state there known as the Shiftings, in which a man's nature "is reversed" [V, 231]). Further, Cuchulain Comforted lacks the full structural support of the Comedy, in which Dante's placement of an episode itself directs exegesis. Yeats's lyric counterpart to the architectonics of epic must rely as best it can on reflections from other Cuchulain works, related imagery elsewhere—for instance, the bird and singing school of Byzantium—and its placement within the volume. Scholars have increasingly realized the thematic importance of Yeats's arrangement of poems within each book. In this case his manuscript list, discovered only after the present arrangement had been set posthumously, indicates that Cuchulain Comforted would have come fourth in a volume moving from the supernatural determinism and escape of Under Ben Bulben to the choice for reimmersion in experience of The Circus Animals' Desertion.[33] Even Cuchulain's acceptance of his new role in the poem prepares for that movement in ratifying by implication his "violent and famous" life on earth. In this respect Yeats's poem inverts the relation between life and death that would shortly inform the only comparable modern work, the Dantesque passage in Part 2 of Little Gidding. Whereas

Eliot presents a bleak picture of natural senescence in implied contrast to supernatural salvation hereafter, Yeats projects a melancholy but acquiescent view of the afterlife which exalts by contrast Cuchulain's heroic life on earth.

In his crucial late tribute to Dante, Yeats himself emerges as the perfected romantic poet of his prose criticism. First, he has grounded his vision securely in Irish lore. The figure of Cuchulain carries the national particularity for which Yeats praised Dante in contrast to Blake. Second, he adopts the dialectic of the antiself which he found lacking in Keats. Not only does Cuchulain himself form a mask for Yeats, but he also here turns into his own antiself by joining the gregarious cowards instead of remaining a solitary hero. And finally, the poem displays the Vision of Evil which Yeats excoriated Shelley for lacking. Acceptance permeates the poem, as both Yeats and his hero accept the ignoble end of the noble warrior as a necessary working out of destiny. Cuchulain's willing submission strengthens both the sorrow of his present lot and the grandeur of his former state. Yeats as author at last saw all things set in order. He could now boast even more truly than he had in *The Tower*:

> I have prepared my peace
> With learned Italian things.

NOTES

1. W. B. Yeats, *Autobiographies* (London: Macmillan, 1966), pp. 114–115. Hereafter cited as *A*. Yeats's response was not unusual. In *Rossetti* (London: Duckworth, 1902), p. 38, Ford Madox Ford took a more guarded view of the important effect of this picture. "The fact remains that, after having seen the picture, this episode of Dante's life must be visualized by men of our time, in a place and with figures like those of Rossetti's," wrote Ford. "And this implies a great deal." For a reproduction of the painting, see the frontispiece of the present volume.

2. See, for example, the discussion of the *Vita Nuova* in T. S. Eliot, *Selected Essays* (New York: Harcourt, Brace & World, 1964), p. 235. Eliot repeatedly contrasts Dante and the romantics.

3. As quoted by F. P. Wilson, "A Supplement to Toynbee's *Dante in English Literature*," in *Italian Studies* 3 (1946): 50–64. Wilson's work supplements Paget Toynbee's immense *Dante in English Literature from Chaucer to Cary*, 2 vols. (London: Methuen,

1909), which reprints every mention of Dante he could find by an English man of letters. For the convenience of the reader, I have cited Wilson and Toynbee in preference to a variety of separate texts.

4. Toynbee, 1:255.

5. Toynbee, 1:341.

6. See Oswald Doughty, "Dante and the English Romantic Poets," *English Miscellany* 2 (1951): 136. Byron was less enthusiastic. For Blake's reading of Cary and knowledge of Dante see Albert S. Roe, *Blake's Illustrations to the Divine Comedy* (Princeton: Princeton University Press, 1953), pp. 4, 6, 30–34.

7. E. H. Plumptre, trans., *The Commedia and Canzoniere of Dante Alighieri*, 2 vols. (London: Wm. Ibister, 1887), 2:440. Plumptre was Dean of Wells and himself a translator of Dante.

8. W. B. Yeats, *Mythologies* (London: Macmillan, 1962), p. 329. Hereafter cited as M. Yeats knew other translations as well. All quotations from Dante in the present essay come from versions known to Yeats or, where certain identification is lacking, at least from those accessible to him.

9. Charles Lancelot Shadwell, trans. *The Purgatory of Dante Alighieri* (London: Macmillan, 1892), p. xiv; hereafter cited as Shadwell. Other quotations in this paragraph may be found on pp. xvii, xix, xxiii. Voltaire had written in the *Dictionnaire Philosophique* that "sa réputation s'affermira toujours parcequ'on ne le lit guère." In William J. De Sua, *Dante into English: A Study of the Translations of the Divine Comedy in Britain and America* (Chapel Hill: University of North Carolina Press, 1964), p. 77, De Sua calls Shadwell "the best poetic translation of the late 19th century," but in Gilbert F. Cunningham, *The Divine Comedy into English: A Critical Bibliography 1782–1900* (Edinburgh and London: Oliver and Boyd, 1965), p. 186, Cunningham cautions that Shadwell's stanzas "form a very poor guide for the reader whose knowledge of the *Comedy* can be obtained only from an English translation." Citations from Cary's translation in this essay come from Henry Francis Cary, trans. and ed., *The Vision; or Hell, Purgatory, and Paradise, of Dante Alighieri* (London: George Bell and Sons, 1889); hereafter cited as Cary.

10. *Uncollected Prose of W. B. Yeats*, ed. John P. Frayne (New York: Columbia University Press, 1970), pp. 251–52; hereafter cited as Uncoll. As usual when mentioning Dante, Yeats went on to discuss romantic poets, in this case Blake and Shelley.

11. W. B. Yeats, *Essays and Introductions* (New York: Macmillan, 1961), p. 140. Hereafter cited as E&I.

12. *The Works of William Blake: Poetic, Symbolic, and Critical*, ed. Edwin John Ellis and William Butler Yeats, 3 vols. (London: Bernard Quaritch, 1893), 1:137–40; *Poems of William Blake*, ed. W. B. Yeats (London: Lawrence and Bullen, 1893), p. xlvi.

13. The eight included the watercolors of *The Passing of Dante and Virgil through the Portico of Hell; Angry Spirits Fighting in the Waters of the Styx; Antaeus Setting Virgil and Dante*

upon the Verge of Cocytus; Dante and Uberti; Dante and Virgil Climbing to the Foot of the Mountain of Purgatory; Dante, Virgil and Statius; The Car of Beatrice; and John Linnell's tracing of Blake's drawing for The Car Following the Seven Candlesticks. For Yeats's projected use of the Paolo and Francesca as frontispiece to Ideas of Good and Evil see The Letters of W. B. Yeats, ed. Allan Wade (London: Rubert Hart-Davis, 1954), p. 377; hereafter cited as Lett.

14. Arthur Symons, Savoy 8 (December 1896): 92.

15. Yeats, Uncollected Prose, p. 141. The following quotations come from pp. 284, 328.

16. The Variorum Edition of the Poems of W. B. Yeats, ed. Peter Allt and Russell K. Alspach (New York: Macmillan, 1966), p. 125. Hereafter cited as VP.

17. The Variorum Edition of the Plays of W. B. Yeats, ed. Russell K. Alspach (New York: Macmillan, 1966), p. 168.

18. W. B. Yeats, Explorations (New York: Macmillan, [1963]), p. 190. Hereafter cited as E.

19. W. B. Yeats, Memoirs, ed. Denis Donoghue (London: Macmillan, 1972), p. 248. Cf. Memoirs, p. 247: "Dante is said to have unified Italy," and E&I, p. 341.

20. Allen R. Grossman, Poetic Knowledge in the Early Yeats: A Study of "The Wind Among the Reeds" (Charlottesville: University of Virginia Press, 1969).

21. W. B. Yeats and T. Sturge Moore: Their Correspondence 1901–1937, ed. Ursula Bridge (London: Routledge and Kegan Paul, 1953), p. 38. Since the subject of Yeats's letter is his hawk symbol, I have added bird to the list.

22. Thomas Vance, "Dante, Yeats, and Unity of Being," Shenandoah 17 (1965):83.

23. Yeats knew Boccaccio's life of Dante; for example, he quotes his remark that "Always both in youth and maturity [Dante] found room among his virtues for lechery" (M, p. 330). In the same place Yeats quoted Rossetti's translation of Guido Cavalcanti's reproach to Dante. The conjunction of an "apple" on a "bough" out of reach occurs in Shadwell's version of Purgatory 27, "That apple sweet, from bough to bough / By man so dearly sought" (Shadwell, 407). I owe this last point to my student, David Spurr, who has written a useful essay on "A Celtic Commedia: Dante in Yeats's Poetry," Rackham Literary Studies (Spring, 1977), 99–116.

24. E, 250. Cf. W. B. Yeats, A Vision (New York: Macmillan, 1958), p. 289, hereafter cited as V. All quotations from A Vision come from that text, except for passages deleted from the original 1925 version (London: T. Werner Laurie), hereafter cited as 1925V.

25. For other instances see E&I, pp. 483, 509; E, p. 356; A, p. 190; and V, pp. 258, 291.

26. Elizabeth Price Sayer, trans., Il Convito: the Banquet of Dante Alighieri (London: George Routledge and Sons, 1887), pp. 126, 156.

27. George Bornstein, Yeats and Shelley (Chicago and London: University of Chi-

cago Press, 1970), pp. 199–218; pp. 218–22 discuss the relationship between Shelley and Yeats as critics of Dante. The quotation about Shelley shaping Yeats's life is from E&I, p. 424.

28. Yeats also compares Dante and Villon in E&I, p. 349 and A, p. 310. Hugh Witemeyer and I have discussed his view of Villon in more detail in "From Villian to Visionary: Pound and Yeats on Villon," Comparative Literature 19 (Fall, 1967):308–20. For other references to Dante and Balzac than those below see E&I, p. 446 and E, pp. 269, 277.

29. Besides those discussed elsewhere in this essay, the "emerald eyes" of The Mask may derive from those of Beatrice in Purgatory 31, the butterflies of Blood and the Moon from that in Purgatory 10, the sighing in News for the Delphic Oracle from that in Inferno 4, the "water, herb and solitary prayer" of Ribh at the Tomb of Baile and Aillinn from the end of Purgatory 22, and Rocky Face of The Gyres from the figure of Dante among others. Why Should Not Old Men Be Mad refers to "a girl that knew all Dante once." David R. Clark, W. B. Yeats and the Theatre of Desolate Reality (Dublin: The Dolmen Press, 1965), pp. 21–25, has suggested that the plays The Dreaming of the Bones, The Words upon the Window-pane, and Purgatory all draw upon the Paolo and Francesca episode. Giorgio Melchiori devotes considerable space to the relation of the story originally known as "The Vision of O'Sullivan the Red" to Dante in his helpful survey, "Yeats and Dante," English Miscellany 19 (1968):153–79. In the chapter on Yeats in his recent Dante and English Poetry: Shelley to T. S. Eliot (Cambridge: Cambridge University Press, 1983), Steve Ellis traces Yeats's fondness for the adjective "pearl-pale" back to Rossetti's description of Beatrice. Finally, Tilottama Rajan in "The Romantic Backgrounds of Yeats's Use of Dante in 'Ego Dominus Tuus,'" Yeats Eliot Review 7 (1982):120–22, suggests that Carlyle may be an important filter for the impact of Dante on that poem.

30. Yeats had gotten into trouble by using Christian symbols in The Countess Cathleen, which we have already seen drew upon Dante. Recalling the protests that the play was anti-Catholic, Yeats wrote that "in using what I considered traditional symbols I forgot that in Ireland they are not symbols but realities" (A, p. 416).

31. Because of its similarity to Yeats in phrasing, I have quoted here from William Michael Rossetti's translation, The Comedy of Dante Alighieri: Part I—The Hell (London and Cambridge: Macmillan, 1865), p. 4. For the early drafts see Jon Stallworthy, Between the Lines: W. B. Yeats's Poetry in the Making (Oxford: Clarendon Press, 1963), chapter 6. The following quotation about flames comes from p. 123.

32. F. A. C. Wilson, W. B. Yeats and Tradition (New York: Macmillan, 1958), p. 246; T. R. Henn, The Lonely Tower: Studies in the Poetry of W. B. Yeats (London: Methuen, 1965), p. 338; Helen Vendler suggests a syntactic parallel between Inferno 15 and the prose draft of Yeats's poem, in Yeats's Vision and the Later Plays (Cambridge, Mass.: Harvard University Press, 1963), p. 247. For the prose version of the poem see

Dorothy Wellesley, ed., *Letters on Poetry from W. B. Yeats to Dorothy Wellesley* (London: Oxford University Press, 1964), p. 193.

33. The list is reprinted in Curtis Bradford, "The Order of Yeats's *Last Poems*," *Modern Language Notes* 76 (1961):515–16. Richard J. Finneran's recent *The Poems of W. B. Yeats: A New Edition* (New York: Macmillan, 1983) properly follows the order of Yeats's own list.

Ezra Pound's Commedia

I

A poem, like a poet, must make its way in the world, undergoing what T. S. Eliot in another connection called "the damage of a lifetime." Ezra Pound's long poem commenced its public life unluckily, its fortunes entangled with those of two better-known works, *The Waste Land* and *Ulysses*. Pound's poem differs profoundly from each of these, but his first readers did not apprehend the difference profoundly. Sensing only that it was there, they concluded that it signified something wrong with the *Cantos*.

The Waste Land, as Eliot remarked to Stephen Spender, "could not have been written at any moment except when it was written": just at that moment in the poet's own life, just at that moment in the story of Europe—one of those moments when, in Spender's phrase, "the long result of time" seems to "come out like a sum."[1] To discern, in the heart of the poem's luminescence, which substances were of private origin, which of public, our most refined spectroscopy must fail, united as they are in fueling the baleful glow. But no fusion of that order unifies the *Cantos*, which by their very nature could only have been written over many years. The work implies no ideal moment of utterance, no date when all flowed into one vatic vision. Instead it tells us that "there is no substitute for a lifetime."

As for *Ulysses*, it was for many decades the paradigm of a complicated modern work. In the very year—1930—in which *A Draft of XXX Cantos* was first published, Stuart Gilbert explained at book length how the Homeric parallel worked in Joyce's hands, and how plausibly a single principle, or perhaps a few principles compatible with one another, could be made to account for the shaping and locating of every Dublin detail.[2] In the ensuing talk about "the mythological method" (a phrase Eliot had coined some years earlier) it seemed not to be remembered that epic parallels had been manipulated before, by Fielding for instance and by Pope, though with less show of rigor, nor to be considered that the more the rigor that obtained, the more surely the presence of such parallels denoted a comic art. No, rigor of correspondence got exalted as the modern discovery, a frame moreover on which to stretch the skins of large solemn creations, and it was clear that the *Cantos*, which seemed to want to be like the *Odyssey* and the *Divine Comedy* at the same time without either system of correspondence ever quite working, could safely be dismissed as a hopeless botch, though with fine bits here and there.

Yet the poem won't go away, and today attracts a critical literature that despite the late start commences to rival in extent what is written about Eliot and Joyce. And the name of Dante goes on being mentioned, though a structural parallel is no longer expected.[3] Dante, the poem lets us understand, has something intimate to do with its shaping, Dante to whom the young Pound devoted the climactic chapter of his first book of prose, *The Spirit of Romance*, in which Homer receives little mention. (Even the Homeric overture—Canto I—is as we shall see an aspect of the invocation of Dante.)

How Dante's *Commedia* might be held as a whole in the mind was a question that was occupying Pound as far back as 1910. "A great mystery play," he suggested, "or better, a cycle of mystery plays"; at any rate not an "epic."[4] The fact that he didn't attribute the *Commedia*'s integrity to its narrative helps explain his own willingness to project a long poem without one. And how the *Cantos* might become a whole was a question that occupied him most of his life. His poem's use of Homer was one unifying tactic. But in its way of thinking about itself it is apt to be guided by its author's thought about Dante.

II

Pound's long poem commences with Homer, concerning whom one of its primary data is this, that Dante had never read him. Latin works purporting to stem from the Greek of Dares Phrygius and Dictys Cretensis circulated in Dante's time, but the Florentine never allows us to forget that his main quarry of Homeric lore was the *Aeneid* of Virgil, whose speaking, moving author he took for his guide to two of the three worlds after this one. Virgil in the sixth book of his *Aeneid* had conducted Aeneas down into the underworld, reshaping a tradition he received from the eleventh book of the *Odyssey*, where Odysseus pays his visit to the shades. So Virgil stood in a double sense between two worlds: between the world of men who breathe and the world of the dead, between the living Italy of Dante and what Dante could hardly begin to imagine, Homer's archaic cosmos where Circe can enchant your ship and the dead crave blood.

There was a tacit "repeat in history" here, the sort of parallel Pound liked to meditate, since he too had had the experience of perceiving through another man's skewed delineations an ancient literature he couldn't read and didn't even have texts for. That was in 1914–15, when he made the English poems of *Cathay* after poems in classical Chinese, a language as closed to him as Greek to Dante. His Virgil had been the art historian Ernest Fenollosa, who himself had studied the poems not in China but at the feet of teachers in Japan. Pound's headnote to *Cathay* speaks of these teachers' "decipherings," as though T'ang dynasty meanings were today as nearly beyond recall as Greek ones had seemed in trecento Tuscany.

Into Tuscany after the fall of Byzantium, though, Byzantine scholars were to come wandering with their manuscript books and their lore about the meanings of words, bringing the Latin west what the West had forgotten even to wish for—Homer's text and the art of reading it. But for them, there would have been no Greek classrooms in Pennsylvania for the adolescent Ezra Pound to meet Homer in.

So Pound's poem commences with *Odyssey* 11, for this reason among others, that *Odyssey* 11 was the seed of the *Inferno*, its availability the most dramatic literary event of the two centuries that followed Dante's death. And as between Dante's journey and Odysseus's journey Virgil's Latin had stood as intermediary, so between Canto I and Homer's Greek (which Pound after all could read) there is made to stand something Latin also, a Renaissance crib prepared by one of those scholars from the East. We are to remember that the matter of an underworld journey, the *Nekuia*, has already received transformation after transformation: has survived, even, the loss and recovery of Homer's rendition. Andreas Divus, whom it names, is one of many who have transformed it; his Latin, dated 1538, was printed to accompany page for page the Aldine Greek text, guiding Renaissance readers not, as Virgil guided Dante, to general themes, but to the intimate sense of the Greek.

Beginning in medias res, "And then went down to the ship," the Canto ends with an open-ended "So that:", to set unspecified consequences reverberating in the silence during which we turn the page. One of these consequences was the Hellenizing enthusiasm of the Renaissance, which helps make a Poliziano's intellectual world feel so different from Dante's. But "So that:" is also written for readers who do not need to be told that a principal consequence of the *Nekuia* was the *Inferno*.

And since what follows "So that:" in the book we are holding is all the rest of the poem, another of the *Nekuia*'s consequences will be the *Cantos*. This is a delicate hint, the poem's second, that it means to bear some analogy with the *Commedia*. (The first such hint has often been noted: it is the poem's title.) "And then went down to the ship," consequently, connotes a going down to (among other ships) the ship that is one of Dante's images for his own poem: the ship from which, at the opening of *Paradiso* 2, he calls back to his reader who trails in a "piccioletta barca." "You in the dinghy (piccioletta) astern there!" comes a similar voice out of the *Cantos*, hailing the reader at the very end of *Thrones*. The tow rope, this voice seems to assure us, has not parted, and the voyage has, despite appearances, been going somewhere, and the skipper is awake.

III

Dante in all this is a precedent and a point of reference. For Pound he is the supreme example of a poet who did what the very young Pound aspired to do: inherited, by diligence as much as by insight, all that was available for him to inherit and summarized much that need not be summarized again. Thus one reason Pound in his twenties and thirties studied the troubadours so intensively was that Dante had studied them and commented on them and made his own the example of their intricate art. Learning from them was a way of learning to emulate Dante. And against the grain of all modern Provençal scholarship, he took the trouble to work word by word, repeatedly, through Arnaut Daniel's knotted and elliptical verses because Dante had commended Daniel above all other troubadours. It is doubtful whether he would have taken this trouble—the kind of trouble that he later wouldn't accord *Finnegans Wake*—had he not credited Dante's certification of *il miglior fabbro*.

This may be the unique case of a modern student believing that the judgments in the *De Vulgari Eloquentia* and elsewhere in the Dante canon could simply be trusted. Scholars generally throw up their hands and their round eyes in wonderment that Dante can possibly have held such opinions. Pound, for whom intelligence was indivisible, thought that the author of the *Divina Commedia* was *prima facie* a more reliable critic of poetry than Professor X.

Part of Dante's credibility, in the early years when young Pound was learning to trust him, would have stemmed from the evident applicability of the *De Vulgari* to the plight of what Pound was to call "U.S. verse," whose practitioners studied a sub-Tennysonian English as assiduously as any trecento Tuscan emulated the surfaces of unsuitable models. It was encouraging to gather from Dante that such a situation had occurred before. All his life Pound was to think of the English of England as analogous to postclassical pseudo-Latin: a remote, muffled, obfuscatory idiom to be combated as Dante combated unsatisfactory writing in his own day, by drawing on any discoverable precedent for the knowing marshaling of spoken sounds.

And if situations recur so may futures; by 1912 Pound thought that all signs pointed to "the imminence of an American Risorgimento."[5] Responsibilities recur as well, and he felt that he had incurred some of Dante's. The *Don'ts for Imagists* (1914) is his *De Vulgari Eloquentia*, the *Jefferson and/or Mussolini* of two decades later perhaps his *De Monarchia*. And the long poem as he meditated it acquired an obligation like Dante's to take stock of the cultural heritage, especially as the principal themes that had entered western history since the *Commedia* was written. That was how visitors of about 1950 heard him explain the poem's principle of inclusion. Its scope was *what had happened since Dante*. That is one of the things we are to gather when it displays Homer being recovered with the help of a crib dated 1538.

IV

The principal themes, then, of western experience since Dante's time: what might they be?

Pound took them to include (1) the Renaissance in Europe, splendid, flawed, volatile, in part the flower of events like the recovery of Homer, in part the manifestation of passions Dante reproves, in part the theater of mysterious disruptions we had better investigate lest we replay not only the inceptions but the anticlimaxes; (2) the story of America, coinvolved in Europe's imagination with China ever since Columbus stumbled on the one while in search of the other; (3) the invention and speedy misuse of centralized finance, which altered men's very conception of scale, responsibility, morality, reward. These are among the *Cantos*'s main themes.

They are inherent but hidden in the opening pages, and the oblique way they are present there helps illustrate the impracticality, for Pound, of Dante's serial presentation, topic following topic in a narrative schema. Thus Odysseus voyaging had been a subject of Dante's Odysseus sailing after knowledge (as though out to discover America) but wrecked instead near Mt. Purgatory for his presumption and now speaking in a hell devised by Eternal Justice, very different from the hell where Homer had him visit Tiresias. In the *Cantos*, Pound's Seafarer-idiom reflection of Divus's reflection of Homer's text reminds us that Pound, as creator of that idiom, is himself reflected by his poem's Odysseus-figure (the *Cantos* first-person in myth if not in grammar), and that when he too went a-sailing after knowledge it was on a ship that set out from America, back toward Europe (the underworld) where, as Canto 7 will reveal, the Tiresias who preceded him and awaits him is (on one plane) Henry James:

And the great domed head *con gli occhi onesti e tardi*
Moves before me, phantom with weighted motion,
Grave incessu, drinking the tone of things . . .[6]

This shade is presented drinking like Homer's Tiresias, though drinking not sheep's blood but "the tone of things," and the "endless sentence" he weaves seems a nobler imposition than the mythological rope of sand. He is the James Pound met in 1913, also a Tiresias, a Good Pagan, a Sordello, a ghost like his own many ghosts, and the emblematic inhabitant of a spectral London where "old men's voices" fill voids amid a dim simulated elegance. (Finance having tainted the leasehold, marble is "false" and paneled wood "suggested.") No person, no situation in the *Cantos* is a univocal archetype, nor is any single presentation complete (James in Canto VII is one projection of Tiresias in Canto I). An Odysseus, a reverse Columbus, a playing out of a Jamesian American Theme, these are among the ways we are encouraged to take the first Canto's autobiographical theme alone. There is no way to sort out such fusions in narrative sequence.

Centralized finance presented unique difficulties. It proved inextricable from the Renaissance, which has defined much of our sense of poetic possibility, and yet getting it into a poem entailed altering radically Pound's readers' sense of what a poem could assimilate. Attempting this in his prose, he often adduced precedents from Dante, reminding us, for instance, how low in the Italian's cone-shaped hell are the usurers and the fraudulent, or affirming that Dante's hell, all its lower part, "reeks with money." Though this last claim has been jeered at it is not only true but is what one should expect of a poet who took seriously the text, *Radix malorum est cupiditas*.

In his distressed old age Pound was to murmur that this text came closer to the mark than he had, that he had mistaken a symptom for a cause, that the real crime was not Usura but Avarice. But when the poem was alive in his mind he was preoccupied with Usura precisely because of its irreversible novelty. Its technologies were post-Dantean, as much so as those of atomic fission.[7] It was not the Usura practiced by such moneylenders as the ones Dante's contemporaries tried to regulate, though Pound used the Latin word to invoke a tradition of medieval excoriation called Usura, "the beast with a hundred legs," like some gargoyle from the *Inferno*, and borrowed the rhetoric of Canto 45—

> with usura, sin against nature,
> is thy bread ever more of stale rags,
> is thy bread dry as paper   [45/229]

—from that devised by the King James translators for Hebraic teachers of doom.

But he was not talking about what Dante would have understood by Usura. He was talking about the practice of creating the whole money supply of a country, of the world, in the form of interest-bearing debt. This was a post-Dantescan mischief, fruit of a novel technology, because in Dante's time there could be no such thing as the money supply of a country. That depended on printing to multiply banknotes, national sovereignty to back them, and easy communications to disseminate them. Reality had tended to keep the pre-Gutenberg moneylender relatively honest, even when he overcharged the borrower. He could only lend you gold coins if he had them, or else he could write you a note, which, even if it corresponded to no gold coins he could lay hands on, still bore his signature only and limited the scope of fraud to the men who passed it along. State-issued or bank-issued paper changed all that.

There is a long tradition of suspecting paper money in itself; Pope is witty about it in the *Epistle to Bathurst*. Pound did not share this generic distrust. A paper money supply, once printing had made it possible, was potentially a public utility since it need not be limited by an irrelevance, the amount of gold that happened to have been mined. But its existence created a new responsibility, that of regulating the amount. That was Pound's major reason for supporting powerful rulers. For control of the money supply by the wrong hands permitted, he thought, the two predominant evils of modern times. The first evil, recurrent wars, was traceable to the conflict for foreign markets, markets countries need because there is never enough money to buy the product at home. The second evil was a steady lowering of quality to absorb unpayable prices, either by adulterating the artifact ("is thy bread ever more of stale rags") or by discontinuing whole categories of effort because they grow too expensive. His examples included carving intrinsic with the stone building and pictures that could not be meant for speculative sale because they were part of the plaster wall. It was with a sense of maintaining a medieval tradition of fiscal ethics that he hammered at such matters, taking Dante on fraud as literally as he took Dante on Arnaut Daniel.

Stone houses, frescoes, those are Renaissance preoccupations, meant to fix the new evil's time of origin. And Usura is a medieval Latin word, meant to name its continuity with older evils. The name applies only by transference to what Pound was talking about. For the modern villain is anonymous, invisible, maybe not even a person but simply a system, though Pound tended to lurch accusingly toward persons. Perhaps a false analogy with the *Inferno* made trouble, for a hell contains persons, not systems, and Dante accordingly specifies sinners by name. In the so-called Hell Cantos (14 and 15) names have been eaten away, and Pound was later to confess that he'd forgotten who some of them were. The considered judgment these Cantos pass on the 1920s is that the time yields no more than a comic-book Inferno, "without dignity, without tragedy." But Pound's urge to fix responsibility, no less than the example of Dante naming names, prevented him from leaving it at that. The black lines in Canto 52 obliterate what had been in typescript a pseudonym for the Rothschilds, on whom he had meant to pin personal responsibility until the publisher's lawyers prevented him, and when Pound did that he merely sounded obsessed.

V

An obsessed Pound haunts the *Cantos*, but so do other Pounds; we have seen that he is one facet of his own Odysseus. For the poet to figure in his own narrative poem appears to be a postclassical possibility not available to Homer or Virgil but exploited by Chaucer and Dante. As Dante Alighieri is a principal character in his *Commedia*, so Ezra Pound is a salient presence in his *Cantos*, notably in the unforeseeable *Pisan Cantos*, where his imprisonment and his memories provide the materials for 115 consecutive pages. When contingent emergencies deflected the poem's course in this way, the poem could accommodate them, because from its conception it had contained the biography of its author. "I sat on the Dogana's

steps," Canto 3 commences, "for the gondolas cost too much, that year."
Caught in the fluctuation of a price system, he can't afford (1908 or so) to
go down to the ship, Odysseus stranded for lack of some Circe's craft.

His intention had been to make an exemplum of his own life, writing
his poem as it were in public, hoping to become the poet who could
write its final passages, trusting too that events would supply, perhaps in
the new Italy, a public *paradiso*.

Here an analogy with the *Commedia* is especially instructive. Dante too
had offered his own plight for exemplum, his journey through death's
kingdoms resembling his exile, his cult of Beatrice Portinari allegorized
in a way that has fed thought for six centuries. But Dante schematized his
facts before he used them. Planning the work with an eye for canonical
symmetries, he chose for his life's midpoint and the date of his vision the
year he was 35, in 1300. It seems not worth asking whether the spring of
that year had in fact contained any notable experiences. It sufficed that
the year inaugurated a century, and that 35 was half of 70, the psalmist's
allotted span though not in those times an actuary's. (Dante was to leave
14 years of it unlived, and by his era's chances his was a long life.)

Pound had commenced a similar self-allegorizing before the *Cantos*
were properly under way, but as usual our discussion, like his treatment,
is complicated by his trust in the obdurate given. He turned thirty-five in
1920, the year of the second part of *Mauberley*, the year he decided to live
no longer in England. That those were months of crisis (*che la diretta via era
smarrita*) he determined not with numerological aid, but from events.
Not only had appalling public events wrecked Europe, he now doubted
his own trajectory. "E. P." had, perhaps not unjustly, "passed from men's
memory," an event he dated in "*l'an trentiesme de son eage*," his thirtieth year,
1915, the year of *Cathay*. In later printings of *Mauberley* this was altered to
"*l'an trentuniesme*," 1916, the year of *Lustra*. Previous to that,

> For three years, out of key with his time,
> He strove to resuscitate the dead art
> Of poetry; to maintain "the sublime"
> In the old sense . . .

In the poem he allows his putative British obituarist (dropper of classical
tags, improviser of meandering sentences) to interject "Wrong from the
start" and then half retract this judgment with

No, hardly, but seeing he had been born
In a half-savage country, out of date . . .

Whether "wrong from the start" or no, by 1920 a wrongness in his life's course preoccupied him, and though he was to outlive the threescore and ten of the Psalmist by more years (seventeen) than Dante fell short of it, still it was at age thirty-five, like Dante, that he judged his life to be in medial entanglement and took the extreme step of compounding exile from America with exile from London.

And he dates the trouble from "three years" before 1915 (or 1916): from 1912, the year of *Ripostes*, or 1913, the year he received the Fenollosa manuscripts and also invented Imagism. With every allowance made for a "half-savage" birthplace, still those three years, the years of *Cathay* and *Noh*, are marked (says his elegist) by some misapprehension of time, of the meaning of time's moving arrow: "out of date," "out of key with his time," oblivious to "the mottoes on sun-dials" (which mark our shadows' irrevocable flight); in fact "unaffected by the 'march of events.'" Events march, like armies. He should have been aware of this.

He had not been, in part because his underlying sense of time was Neoplatonic.[8] An early poem, *The Flame*, is emphatic in rejecting "'days and nights' and troubling years"; "the net of days and hours," it says, can be eluded. In vision men can be one with "the ever-living," and it is the calling of poetry to transmit intimations of this ecstasy. Time is the enemy: an ever rolling stream. Those ideal conceptions toward the contemplation of which the mind aspires belong outside of time and fall into time as into a torrent. As we read in *Cathay*,

At morning there are flowers to cut the heart,
And evening drives them on the eastward-flowing waters.

Time is the tireless undoer:

Time is the evil. Evil

—an evil for young Pedro to defy by exhuming a corpse,

dead eyes,
Dead hair under the crown,
The King still young there beside her.   [30/147–48]

Pound was 59 when this incident from Canto 30 was rhymed in Pisa, memory setting up another face:

> Time is not, Time is the evil, beloved
> Beloved the hours βροδοδάκτυλοσ
> > as against the half-light of the window
> > with the sea beyond making horizon
> le contre-jour the line of the cameo
> profile "to carve Achaia"
> > a dream passing over the face in the half-light   [74/444]

"Time is the evil," countered here by a rare moment when "time is not." Perfection is exempt from time until time claims it, and happenings are undoings. If the reader is admonished in a very late Canto—

> You forget the timing of budgets
> > that is to say you probably don't even know that
> Officials exist in time. You are fairly unconscious   [99/706]

—still the time there designated is cyclical, bringing springs and harvests.

> (the k'ao ch'eng is according to harvest,
> the tax as a share of something produced.   [99/706]

That is not time but recurrence.

But "a poem including history" cannot simply evade time's irreversible arrow (whose barb—"the barb of time"—furnishes Canto 5 with a celebrated image). So to the three main conventions of the poem, the journey, the metamorphosis, the revery, exemplified one at a time in the first three Cantos, Pound added a fourth, the chronicle adumbrated in the Malatesta sequence (Cantos 8–11), and conceived for the whole work a tripartite division analogous to Dante's. *Inferno, Purgatorio, Paradiso*: he affords no point-for-point correspondence here, rather a hint taken from the fact that only in the purgatorial sector of Dante's afterworld can anything be said to change.[9] In Hell souls suffer in fixity, locked into an unchanging now for which Dante's image is an inescapable location, a numbered circle, bounded. In Paradise unaltering souls are whelmed in their proper allotment of the pervading light. But in purgatory, souls change; they enter this place unworthy, they leave it cleansed; and if the action of the *Commedia* is Dante's journey, if he lingers with souls in Purgatory only for moments, leaving them behind as though they were fixed in their suffering, he alone free to depart, still he does not allow his readers to forget that in Purgatory slow change takes place, that a stay here has a finite duration, measured in time.

Pound offered an ingenious secular analogy. A poem of vivid static scenes launched with the momentum of a sea journey, disregards chronology or consistency of locale until in Canto 52 the scene shifts decisively to China. The time of cyclical recurrence is next invoked, the summer-to-winter half of a ceremonial calendar with its natural signs and prescribed observances. Thereupon the poem plunges into an element it has hitherto shunned, the extended chronicle-time of history. It is now the reader's destiny to commence a long story at the very beginning and gather his rewards by staying alert.

> Yeou taught men to break branches
> Seu Gin set up the stage and taught barter,
>   taught the knotting of cords
> Fou Hi taught men to grow barley
>   2837 ante Christum
> and they know still where his tomb is
> by the high cypress between the strong walls . . .   [53/262]

For nine consecutive cantos, 53–61, the chronicle progresses along a temporal arrow, marking the route with dates, from before 2837 B.C. until 1735 A.D.—almost five millennia. Then the pace slows and ten more cantos dilate on the life of John Adams, 1735–1826, the last Emperor in the sequence. A hymn to Zeus (κυβερνῶν—steersman) closes the chronicle. For 164 pages time has broken into the Cantos, as time broke into Dante's scheme when the Commedia turned its attention to Purgatory.

If things do not improve in Pound's historical time, neither do they simply degenerate. Rather, norms are lost and recovered, lost and recovered, the welfare of the folk in China fluctuates, and a record of exemplary experience accumulates. Under Chou (also spelled Chai and Tcheou; alphabets have a clumsy grasp on Chinese sounds),

> Exchange brought abundance, the prisons were empty.
> 'Yao and Chun have returned'
>   sang the farmers

'Peace and abundance bring virtue.' I am
   'pro-Tcheou' said Confucius five centuries later
With his mind on this age.   [53/268]

At another time,

Rice was one mark silver the measure
   in Kaï fong
and human meat sold in market
   Litse's gangsters all over Honan
Li Sao: weep, weep over Kaïfong; Kientsong the bloody
and Litse called himself Emperor   [58/322]

Such times are offered not as myths but as happenings whose causes may
enlighten us. Confucius "five centuries later" looked back to Chou; under
Chou the farmers sang that Yao and Chun had returned; the good by
definition is located in ascertainable experience, recoverable, renewable.
That is one meaning of the injunction "Make It New," which might also
on Pound's showing be a motto for Dante's Purgatory, and surely would
have been had Dante been born in the New World. ("Can't repeat the
past?" Jay Gatsby cried incredulously. "Why of course you can!")

The Chronicle is the second main division of the poem, and the third,
commencing inauspiciously in Pisa, consists of the mind's effort to hold
together a pointillist vision of Paradise. If we choose to call what comes
before the China Chronicle *Inferno* and what comes after it *Paradiso*, we
shall have to enforce the principle of distinction between these two. It is
not obvious; the sinners are not confined to the first section, nor the
saints to the last. As for the poet's own fortunes, they were never lower
than when he undertook to write "Elysium, though it were in the halls of
hell," whereas it is in the infernal part of the schema that we find such
details as the memory (Canto 26) of his young youth, when he lay in
Venice all day taking in the view to the east and proposed to devote
whole future days to the south and southwest.

And at night they sang in the gondolas
And in the barche with lanthorns;
The prows rose silver on silver
   taking light in the darkness.   [26/121]

It is just in such a passage that we may find our clue. They are tourist passages, innocent indulgences in spectacle; they comport with repeated nudges to regard history as a pageant staged "in the arena." And the splendor of Venice comes often but comes in glimpses and flashes, "light in the darkness," dimness hanging in mist, the whole sustained by maritime usury and by endless committee meetings, uncountable regulations. We may note too that Europe's Great War, the wars of the Renaissance, and American modes of commercial degeneracy are ritually intertwined, and that the poem returns less and less indulgently to its repertoire of archetypal events. Baldy Bacon in Canto 12 seems an entertaining rogue with his scheme to buy "all the little copper pennies in Cuba." The Bank of the United States, when the x-ray reveals its exercise of a comparable grip on public funds, is not entertaining in the least. That is what goes on from the opening lines to the threshold of the Chronicle: a long unmasking. Pound remarked in 1948 that the first forty-odd cantos were "a detective story." "Nineteen years on this case," says the dominant voice of Canto 46:

> I have set down part of
> The Evidence. Part/commune sepulchrum
> Aurum est commune sepulchrum. Usura, commune sepulchrum.
> helandros   kai heleptolis   kai helarxe.
> Hic Geryon est. Hic hyperusura.   [46/234–35]

The mutation of the Aeschylean "helandros, kai heleptolis" is characteristic of the infernal phase. The sequence of oracular plays on the name of Helen was carried into Canto 2 by the speech of the waves, a phonemic curiosity to rhyme with another curiosity, the derivation of Eleanor of Aquitaine's name from Helen's. But now, at the close of "the first phase of this opus," the breaker of men and cities and order is no lady in an ancient or medieval story, but "aurum" and "usura." When we first encountered *aurum* (gold) in Canto 1 it furnished Tiresias with a wand and Aphrodite with "girdles and breast-bands," and as for usura, we may have thought it part of a problem that went out with the middle ages. Not so; and the name of Geryon (from *Inferno* 26–27; he is later called "twin with usura") reminds us which part of the *Commedia* is pertinent.

So the history that commenced as a spectacle to beguile a young poet

such as the pre-*Mauberley* Pound has turned into a "case," much of its early
glamor serving to "distract idle minds." Spectacle is barocco and false
fronts. But after the Chinese Chronicle the poem's way of doing its business alters. Where formerly the visionary intellect had described a lei-
sured scene—

> The plain, distance, and in fount-pools
>   the nymphs of that water
> rising, spreading their garlands,
>   weaving their water-reeds with the boughs
> In the quiet,
>   and now one man rose from his fountain
> and went off into the plain.   [16/69–70]

—the energizing mind now draws together clusters of brilliant details.
The nymph, the bough, the water, the fountain (Castalia), these are all in
Canto 90, but held in collocation by nervous visionary force:

> Grove hath its altar
>   under elms, in that temple, in silence
> a lone nymph by the pool.
>   Wei and Han rushing together
> two rivers together
>   bright fish and flotsam
> torn bough in the flood
>   and the waters clear with the flowing
> Out of heaviness where no mind moves at all
>
> .   .   .   .
>
>   the stone under elm
> Taking form now,
>   the rilievi,
>   the curled stone at the marge
> Faunus, sirenes,
>   the stone taking form in the air
>   ac ferae,
>   cervi,
>   the great cats approaching . . .   [90/607–8]

In no normally envisaged landscape do nymph and faun and the Chinese rivers Wei and Han coexist, or stones and cats emerge from void air. They are forced together by the river-like pressure of the visionary faculty asserting itself.

So Pound is doing what he set out to do, becoming the poet who could write the later Cantos, for which the earlier ones have no precedent to offer. It is not a secure achievement; no vision lasts. In Canto 91 a visionary trajectory is suddenly ruptured by obsession, an ugly glob of hate ("How mean thy hates," a voice had said in Pisa), and he lets us see him lose the thread and grope to recover it, soothing his mind for a half-page with memories of Verona until the miraculous birth of Merlin slips once more into place and the ascent resumes. He is not in Paradise, he has only mastered the knack of occasionally glimpsing Paradise, in moments when he can calm his perturbing spirit whose perturbations he knows more bitterly than any critic. "Fear, father of cruelty," he says in Canto 114:

> ubi amor, ibi oculus.
> But these had thrones
>   and in my mind were still, uncontending—
> not to possession, in hypostasis
>   Some hall of mirrors.
>   Quelque toile
> "au Louvre en quelque toile"
>   to reign, to dance in a maze,
> To live a thousand years in a wink ...   [114/793]

And at the end of Canto 116:

> To confess wrong without losing rightness:
> Charity I have had sometimes,
>   I cannot make it flow thru.
> A little light, like a rushlight
>   to lead back to splendour.   [116/797]

NOTES

1. Stephen Spender, T. S. Eliot (New York: Penguin Books, 1976), pp. 117–18.

2. Joyce told Samuel Beckett he could "justify every syllable." "That is one way to write," said Beckett in passing this on, "but it is not the only way."

3. A whole book, James J. Wilhelm's Dante and Pound: The Epic of Judgement (Orono, Maine: University of Maine Press, 1974), has been devoted to their similarities. One in particular, a shared didactic rigor, is much illuminated by Professor Wilhelm's pages.

4. Ezra Pound, The Spirit of Romance (New York: New Directions, 1968), pp. 153–54.

5. Ezra Pound, Selected Essays, ed. William Cookson (New York: New Directions, 1973), p. 111.

6. Dante's Good Pagans move (Inferno 4.112) con occhi tardi e gravi, Sordello (Purgatorio 6.63) de li occhi onesta e tarda. This fusion of Dantescan tags accords James characteristics of them both (see Wilhelm, p. 105). Ezra Pound, The Cantos (New York: New Directions, 1970), p. 24. References are to canto and page number.

7. "A detail," he called the A-Bomb when a visitor (D. G. Bridson) tried to get him excited about radioactive perils. "At my time of life I cannot get bogged down in details."

8. Why this should have been so, thanks how much to temperament, how much to nineteenth-century American idealism, how much to the heritage of Pater via Yeats, would take us too far afield to inquire.

9. However we apply the three divisions, they remain provisional and suggestive. We may note (with Pound, in a letter to his father) that the Hell Cantos proper (14, 15) are followed by a transition through acid baths to an earthly Paradise (see Canto 16, first two pages). We may decide, with Professor Pearlman, to include Cantos 31–71 only in the Purgatory, or take Professor Wilhelm's hint that the Pisan experience was the poet's own Purgatory, a second one, unforeseen. The account I offer here stresses the plain fact that the poem is interrupted by a 4500-year chronicle, after which its texture alters radically. The Letters of Ezra Pound, 1907–1941, ed. D. D. Paige (New York: Harcourt, Brace & World, 1950), p. 210.

STUART Y. McDOUGAL

T. S. Eliot's
Metaphysical Dante

On 4 July 1950, while addressing the Italian Institute in London, T. S. Eliot acknowledged his literary dependence on Dante: "I still, after forty years, regard his poetry as the most persistent and deepest influence on my verse."[1] This influence is easily discernible, for allusions to Dante and citations from the *Commedia* pervade Eliot's poetry, from *The Love Song of J. Alfred Prufrock* to *Four Quartets*. But Dante's impact extends far beyond such important though limited contexts. Gradually, as his understanding of the *Commedia* deepened, Eliot found ways of adapting Dante's poetic strategies to his own uses. He discovered in the *Commedia* a type of poetry which he classified as "metaphysical" and strove increasingly to emulate in his own work. Eliot made Dante the cornerstone of a literary tradition which came to include the poets of the *dolce stil nuovo*, the English metaphysical poets, the French symbolist poets and, of course, Eliot's own work. Significantly, Eliot excluded not only his Romantic and Victorian predecessors in English and American literature from this tradition, but indeed, most of the major English writers since Shakespeare. Confronted with the awesome achievements of his immediate precursors, Eliot turned to the example of a poet temporally and linguistically remote from whom he could learn ways of revitalizing English verse and of purifying the language of the tribe. Dante became a constant influence on Eliot, although the nature of that influence continually changed.

Within the last decade, the availability of manuscripts has encouraged studies of Eliot's development as a poet and a critic. These manuscripts also make it easier to chart the influence of Dante, for they reveal the extent of Eliot's experimentation with different passages from the *Commedia*. Dante's impact on Eliot achieves a new significance when viewed within this larger context.

Although Eliot drew widely from the *Commedia*, one passage exerted a singular fascination for him. Both in manuscripts and in completed poems, Eliot continually alludes to the lines at the conclusion of Canto 26 of the *Purgatorio*, where Arnaut Daniel speaks in Provençal:

> "Tan m'abellis vostre cortes deman,
> qu'ieu no me puesc ni voill a vos cobrire.
> Ieu sui Arnaut, que plor e vau cantan;
> consiros vei la passada folor,
> e vei jausen lo joi qu'esper, denan.
> Ara vos prec, per aquella valor
> que vos guida al som de l'escalina,
> sovenha vos a temps de ma dolor!"
> Poi s'ascose nel foco che li affina.   [140–48]

> (So does your courteous request please me that I neither can nor would conceal myself from you. I am Arnaut, who weep and sing as I go; contritely I see my past folly, and joyously I see before me the joy that I await. Now I pray you, by that power which guides you to the summit of the stair, in due time be heedful of my pain." Then he hid himself in the fire that purifies them.)[2]

Eliot quotes from these lines in the epigraph to an early version of *The Love Song of J. Alfred Prufrock*, and he alludes to them several times in his first book of verse, *Prufrock and Other Observations* (1917). His third volume, *Ara Vos Prec* (1920), takes its title from these lines, and the passage plays a decisive part in his major long poems, *The Waste Land* (1922), *Ash Wednesday* (1930), and *Four Quartets* (1943). Eliot's continuing use of this passage forms a paradigm of his developing view of Dante.

Eliot began studying Dante in 1910, following a Harvard tradition of reading Dante in the original without prior training in Italian. Dante studies had long been important at Harvard, and Eliot paid tribute to two Harvard Professors, C. H. Grandgent and George Santayana, in the preface to *Dante* (1929).[3] Although these critics certainly shaped Eliot's view of Dante, it is difficult to believe that they excited his interest in Arnaut Daniel. C. H. Grandgent speaks of Daniel as "one of the most laborious and tiresome of the Provençal versifiers,"[4] and George Santayana ignores him completely in *Three Philosophical Poets* (1910), a book much admired by Eliot. Eliot's enthusiasm for Daniel was more likely fostered by Ezra Pound's first volume of criticism, *The Spirit of Romance* (1910). We do not know when Eliot obtained this book, but he had probably read it no later than 1914, the year he and Pound first met.

Ezra Pound considered Arnaut Daniel a writer of major stature whose work marked the culmination of the early medieval period. Daniel is one of the key figures in *The Spirit of Romance*. Pound begins his study with a chronological survey of medieval Latin poetry which concludes with a translation of the *Pervigilium Veneris*. The final lines of that poem, recounting the story of Philomel, pose a question:

> Ah, when shall mine own spring come?
> When, as a swallow long silent, shall my silence end?[5]

Pound applies these lines to the early medieval period (chapter 1 is called "The Phantom Dawn") and, paraphrasing the classical scholar John W. Mackail, notes that "song did not again awake until the Provençal viol aroused it" (*Romance*, 21). In the next chapter, Pound carefully examines the songs of Arnaut Daniel which, he suggests, brought this period of silence to an end. Pound begins chapter 2 by noting Dante's lofty praise of Daniel in the *Purgatorio*:

> ... having spoken of Guinizelli as "father of me and of others my betters who ever use sweet and delicate rimes of love," [Dante] says to him: "Your lovely songs as long as modern use shall last will make their very ink precious": and Il Saggio replies, pointing to a spirit before him: "This one whom I point out with my finger was the better craftsman in the mother tongue. He surpassed all verses of love and prose of romances; let fools talk who believe that that fellow from Limoges (Giraut of Bornelh) excels him. To rumor rather than truth they turn their faces, and thus fix their opinion before paying attention to art or reason ... [*Romance*, 23].

Pound does not, however, cite the speech of Daniel which follows in the *Purgatorio*. He is more concerned with the craftsman whose work Dante analyzes in *De Vulgari Eloquentia* than with the figure who suffers in the *Purgatorio*. Most of Pound's chapter is devoted to a consideration of Daniel's verse. The first poem Pound cites is *Sols sui qui sai lo sobrafan quem sorts*, a canzon much admired by Dante and imitated by Pound in a poem of his own. Pound's remarks on the diction of this poem are particularly apposite, for they indirectly clarify Dante's punishment of Daniel "nel foco che li affina." Pound calls our attention to Daniel's use of the verb *esmirar* (refine), noting that "after the comparison of gold and lead, the metal worker's shop gives tribute, and is present to the vision in the technical word 'refine'" (*Romance*, 33). Daniel's choice of verb exemplifies his "terse vigor of suggestion . . . the use of the picturesque verb with an exact meaning" (*Romance*, 33). In a later chapter ("La dolce lingua toscana") Pound observes of Guinizelli's sonnet, "Io vo del ver la mia donna lodare," that "the word 'raffina' recalls a similar line in Arnaut Daniel" (*Romance*, 106). Pound does not elaborate upon the parallel, nor does he mention Dante's use of the same term in the last line of Canto 26 of the *Purgatorio*. However, both Guinizelli and Daniel wrote love poetry describing the effects of beauty on the observer, who became "refined" in the presence of his beloved. Dante's purgatorial flames, which transmute eros into agape, represent the ultimate in refinement. Eliot will later make this idea central to his own poetics.

Eliot began composing *The Love Song of J. Alfred Prufrock* within a year of his first reading of Dante, and Dante's impact was immediate. An early version of the poem with the subtitle (*Prufrock Among the Women*) exists in a notebook of Eliot's now in the Berg Collection at the New York Public Library. It is substantially the same as the final version, although the section beginning "Shall I say, I have gone at dusk through narrow streets" bears the title "PRUFROCK'S PERVIGILIUM" and includes a thirty-five line "pervigilium" of the protagonist from evening to dawn. After copying the poem into the notebook, Eliot added the following epigraph:

> Sovegne vos al temps de mon dolor
> Poi s'ascose nel foco che gli affina.[6]

Already Eliot was seeking a way to use these lines, although he later decided that this was not the place. Why?

Dante opens his epic "nel mezzo del cammin di nostra vita" ("Midway in the journey of our life"), thereby involving the reader ("nostra vita") in a quest which begins in medias res. Eliot commences The Love Song of J. Alfred Prufrock "nel mezzo," the "then" of the first line ("Let us go then") indicating a continuation of an earlier action. Like Dante, Eliot incorporates his reader into his poem: "Let us go then, you and I." However, Eliot's pronouns do not remain fixed: the "you" initially serves as an invitation to the reader and then becomes one of two personae ("you and I") who—like the characters "Dante" and "Virgil" in the Commedia—embark upon a quest. These personae can also be viewed as different aspects of a single psyche.

Two qualities that Eliot was later to praise in Dante's verse distinguish this poem: a "lucidity of style" and "clear visual images" (D, 22). In Eliot's depiction of Prufrock's condition, we are reminded of a remark in Dante (1929): "Hell, though a state, is a state which can only be thought of, and perhaps only experienced, by the projection of sensory images" (D, 32). Long before formulating his critical terminology, Eliot was attempting to find images which were "objective correlatives" for emotions. As Mario Praz has demonstrated, Eliot's notion of the "objective correlative" derives from Pound's discussion of the "objective imagination" of Dante and the Tuscans in The Spirit of Romance.[7] Through Pound, Eliot is beginning to develop an important Dantean strategy in his own work.

In addition, the poem resounds with echoes of Dante, particularly the passage from the Inferno where Dante questions his fitness for such an endeavor:

> Ma io, perché venirvi? o chi 'l concede?
>   Io non Enëa, io non Paulo sono;
>   me degno a ciò né io né altri 'l crede.
> Per che, se del vinire io m'abbandono,
>   temo che la venuta non sia folle.   [2.31–35]

(But I, why do I come here? And who allows it? I am not Aeneas, I am not Paul; of this neither I nor others think me worthy. Wherefore, if I yield and come, I fear that the coming may be folly.)

Prufrock is also engaged on a quest, and the parallels with Dante underline the bathos of his situation. Like Dante, he enters the underworld and compares his task with those who have gone before. But when Dante asks if he "dares" to embark upon such a mission, Virgil assures him that he will receive the support of God's grace on his journey. No such comfort awaits Prufrock. He too asks if he "dare." When the question becomes specific—"Do I dare to eat a peach?"—his quest collapses. The modern world is his inferno, and Prufrock, unable to speak or act, remains trapped within it. His suffering, unlike the agonies of those who find themselves in Purgatory, becomes an end in itself. Later, in *Dante* (1929), Eliot would note that "in the anaesthesia of Virgil is hopelessness" (D, 40), and the same could be remarked of the "anaesthesia" of Prufrock.

Although Eliot's first choice of epigraph indicates his fascination with Arnaut Daniel, it is not consonant with the depiction of Prufrock's predicament. Sensing this, Eliot replaced the purgatorial fires with the quivering flames of the inferno. Guido da Montefeltro speaks:

> "S'i' credesse che mia risposta fosse
>   a persona chi mai tornasse al mondo,
>   questa fiamma staria sanza più scosse;
> ma però che già mai di questo fondo
>   non tornò vivo alcun, s'i' odo il vero
>   sanza tema d'infamia ti rispondo."   [*Inferno* 27, 61–66]

("If I thought that my answer were to one who might ever return to the world, this flame would shake no more; but since from this depth none ever returned alive, if what I hear is true, I answer you without fear of infamy.")

Guido is a proud man, yet he wants to confine the knowledge of his crime to the denizens of hell. Believing Dante to be one of the damned, he confides in him "sanza tema d'infamia." Likewise Prufrock, who is trapped in hell, can communicate with those who share his condition. The epigraph also articulates Prufrock's fears of self-exposure which are expressed throughout the poem, and notably near the end:

> Would it have been worth while . . .
> To say: "I am Lazarus, come from the dead,
> Come back to tell you all, I shall tell you all"—
> If one, settling a pillow by her head,

Should say: "That is not what I meant at all,
    That is not it, at all."

Montefeltro's relationship to Dante parallels Prufrock's relationship to us, as readers of the poem. We are drawn into his world by the invocation of the first line, and we understand his world because its contours are so immediately recognizable. But we escape Prufrock's fate, just as Dante, being human, can escape Montefeltro's.

The *Love Song of J. Alfred Prufrock* is the first of Eliot's poems to be decisively marked by Dante's presence. Although Eliot quickly put his new knowledge of Dante to use, Dante's influence remains rather superficial. Details from the *Inferno* do little more than help establish the poem's topography. This is equally true of the other poems in Eliot's first volume. Allusions and citations from Dante are frequent, but remain less important than Eliot's initial development of the Dantean "objective correlative."

Ara Vos Prec (1920) was Eliot's third and last collection of short poems to be published with significant new material. He took great care in the organization of the volume, as he had with *Prufrock and Other Observations* (1917). Only the poems from *Prufrock and Other Observations*, which concluded the book, remained as originally printed (with the exception of *Hysteria* which Eliot dropped); the six new poems and those from *Poems* (1919) were rearranged to stress the congruity of experience. What Eliot noted of the *Commedia* at this time could be said of his own volume as well: "The artistic emotion presented by any episode . . . is dependent upon the whole."[8] Eliot emphasized this by his choice of title: "*Now I pray you*," the poet implores, "by that power which guides you to the summit of the stair, in due time be heedful of my pain." *Ara Vos Prec* is like a vast tapestry depicting the poet's dolor. What unifies this volume are the violent emotions and feelings, often caused by unfulfilled or misdirected sexual desires, and the sense of pervasive suffering. In addition, the volume is marked by a radical experimentation with language and form. With a diction that is arcane, erudite, and, at times, entirely foreign (i.e., the poems in French), and with the restrictions of the quatrain form, Eliot attempts here to "force, to dislodge if necessary, language into meaning."[9]

Although *Gerontion* is the opening poem in *Ara Vos Prec*, it was the last poem in the volume Eliot composed. Formally, it looks backward to *The Love Song of J. Alfred Prufrock*, but the speaker prefigures Tiresias. Four of the lines from the deleted "PRUFROCK'S PERVIGILIUM" provide an appropriate gloss on the poem:

> And to hear my madness singing, sitting on the kerbstone,
> (A blind old drunken man who sings and mutters,
> With broken boot heels stained in many gutters)
> And as he sang the world began to fall apart . . .

The world of *Gerontion* does more than fall apart: it is finally

> whirled
> Beyond the circuit of the shuddering Bear
> In fractured atoms.

Gerontion's own thoughts scarcely cohere: his mind, like the empty decaying house, can barely contain them. Gerontion resembles those spirits in the *Inferno* who wish not to be recognized, as he reflects on a life characterized by the lack of desire and the failure of love. He defines his life by negations (what he has not done) and by images of sterility and barrenness. The experiences of Gerontion's life which the poem chronicles remain disparate: missing is the catalyst which could produce their unification.

In his notebook in the Berg Collection, Eliot tried out an epigraph from Dante which he ultimately discarded. There we find the words of Fra Alberigo from Canto 33 of the *Inferno*. Dante is astonished to encounter him in hell, for he knows that Alberigo's body is still on earth. He asks Alberigo how he can be with the dead, and Alberigo replies:

> "Come 'l meo corpo stea
> nel mondo sù, nulla scïenza porto."   [33.122–23]
>
> ("How my body may fare in the world above I have no
> knowledge.")

His sin is of such magnitude that his soul has preceded his body to hell. The nameless speaker of *Gerontion* finds that his earthly existence has become a personal hell, but his sins are insignificant compared to those of Alberigo. Like Alberigo, however, he lacks physical definition, a characteristic which links him to Tiresias and contrasts him with the other personae in *Ara Vos Prec*. The other names within the poem equally resemble spirits of the *Inferno*, caught, like Gerontion, in empty rituals now void of all significance. But Eliot's attempt to fuse the different levels of the poem (historical, sexual, religious) is only partially successful. However, the desire to achieve a fusion of sensuality and intellect remains central throughout this volume.

In *Ara Vos Prec*, the quatrain poems are arranged so as to emphasize the tensions developed in *Gerontion*. After *Gerontion*, we encounter *Burbank with a Baedeker: Bleistein with a Cigar*, and we fall immediately into the modern world of vulgar sexuality, contrasted with the timeless values of the classical world. The brutal physicality of sex confronts the reader in *Sweeney Among the Nightingales* and *Sweeney Erect*. Then, with *Mr Eliot's Sunday Morning Service*, the world of Sweeney is contrasted with the empty formalities of religious practices, a preoccupation which is continued with *Whispers of Immortality* and *The Hippopotamus*. *A Cooking Egg*, the last of the quatrain poems is the first of three poems concerned with "de débacles nuptiales," to quote a line of Laforgue's that Eliot cites in his essay on *The Metaphysical Poets*. The potential horrors of marriage and of sexual relations are delineated in *Lune de Miel* (Honeymoon) and most strikingly in *Ode*, the poem which concludes the new section, where a "tortured" bridegroom views the bloodstained sheet with horror. So perverse is the view of sexuality presented here that *Ode* was deleted from the American edition of the volume. *Ode* is particularly interesting because here Eliot fails to achieve the desired transformation of personal material into objective form, a central concern of his in this volume. The first two stanzas remain too autobiographical, with the emotions close to the surface.

> Tired.
> Subterrene laughter synchronous
> With silence from the sacred wood
> And bubbling of the uninspired
> Mephitic river.
>   Misunderstood
> The accents of the now retired
> Profession of the calamus.

Tortured.
When the bridegroom smoothed his hair
There was blood upon the bed.
Morning was already late.
Children singing in the orchard
(Io Hymen, Hymenaee)
Succuba eviscerate.

In the third stanza, Eliot attempts to find an objective correlative for
these feelings and emotions:

Tortuous.
By arrangement with Perseus
The fooled resentment of the dragon
Sailing before the wind at dawn
Golden apocalypse. Indignant
At the cheap extinction of his taking-off
Now lies he there
Tip to tip washed beneath Charles' Wagon.

Taken alone, the third stanza is methodologically similar to entire quatrain poems in its purposeful allusiveness (note the use of astrological
metaphors, frequent in these poems, as they were in the poems of Keats
and Shelley). Eliot's view of Hamlet (published contemporaneously with
this poem) could be applied to Ode as well: it is "full of stuff that the
writer could not drag to light, contemplate, or manipulate into art."[10]
Like Hamlet, Eliot's poem fails because it produces an "intense feeling,
ecstatic or terrible, without an object or exceeding its object" (SE, 126). In
short, Eliot is unable to create the necessary "objective correlative."

Eliot's essay on "The Metaphysical Poets" also sheds light on his poetic
concerns in this volume. Eliot's discussion of "metaphysicality" illuminates his remarks, cited earlier, on creativity. The metaphysical poets,
Eliot notes, were "engaged in the task of trying to find the verbal equivalent for states of mind and feeling" (SE, 248). One finds in their work,
as in the work of their immediate predecessors, "a direct sensuous apprehension of thought, or a recreation of thought into feeling" (SE, 246).
Moreover, the metaphysical poet is able to fuse different elements

together in his work, as Eliot had attempted to do in *Gerontion*. In a now famous example, Eliot asserts: "When a poet's mind is perfectly equipped for its work, it is constantly amalgamating disparate experience; the ordinary man's experience is chaotic, irregular, fragmentary. The latter falls in love, or reads Spinoza, and these two experiences have nothing to do with each other, or with the noise of the typewriter or the smell of cooking; in the mind of the poet these experiences are always forming new wholes" (SE, 247). As though to exemplify this process in his essay, Eliot himself quotes from such disparate "metaphysicals" as Donne and Laforgue, Herbert and Baudelaire. Eliot perceives likenesses in such different poets; the reader, by assenting to Eliot's examples, tacitly accepts Eliot's definition. But more is at stake here than a definition of metaphysicality; Eliot is developing a notion of tradition he had articulated a year earlier:

> The poets of the seventeenth century, the successors of the dramatists of the sixteenth, possessed a mechanism of sensibility which could devour any kind of experience. They are simple, artificial, difficult, or fantastic, as their predecessors were; no less nor more than Dante, Guido Cavalcanti, Guinizelli, or Cino. In the seventeenth century a dissociation of sensibility set in, from which we have never recovered; and this dissociation, as is natural, was aggravated by the influence of the two most powerful poets of the century, Milton and Dryden. [SE, 247]

Eliot discovered the now famous phrase, "the dissociation of sensibility," in an essay by Remy de Gourmont on another of Eliot's favorite writers, Jules Laforgue.[11] Eliot has interpreted the phrase in his own fashion and used it to characterize the decline of verse in England since the Civil War (which, in this essay, he refers to as the Revolution). Eliot has redefined the "direct current of English poetry" (SE, 250) so that his immediate poetic precursors are simply eliminated. In "The Perfect Critic," Eliot remembered Arthur Symons's book, *The Symbolist Movement in Literature*, as "an introduction to wholly new feelings, as a revelation" (SW, 5). It was, in fact, an act of liberation—and what the symbolist poets liberated Eliot from were several centuries of English verse. A similar liberation occurred when Eliot read Dante. Milton and the Romantics, Tennyson and

Browning—the landscape has been cleared. The devastated remains may resemble a waste land, but that is easier to confront than the specters of one's overbearing literary ancestors.

A poem that achieves a tenuous fusion of such intense feelings and simultaneously expresses this view of literary history is *Sweeney Among the Nightingales*. Commentators have gone astray here, as in so many of Eliot's quatrain poems, by seeking a traditional narrative. F. O. Matthiessen has paraphrased Eliot as saying that "all he [Eliot] consciously set out to create . . . was a sense of foreboding."[12] The poem is an objectification, through specific detail, of the emotions which produce this "sense." In a discussion of the "transmutation and transformation" of "passions" into poetry in "Tradition and the Individual Talent," Eliot cites several examples from the *Inferno* where this objectification is successful (Dante's encounter with Brunetto Latini, the voyage of Ulysses, the episode of Paolo and Francesca) and then mentions two other passages which have particular relevance to this poem: the murder of Agamemnon, which is alluded to in the epigraph, and Keats's *Ode to a Nightingale*. Eliot is attempting a similar transmutation in his poem, and his reliance on the attempts of his precursors (even when veiled, as in the case of Keats) is not surprising. Throughout Eliot's poem, the hallucinatory nightmare of Sweeney is implicitly contrasted with the reverie of Keats's speaker. Eliot's poem is in part a dialogue with Keats, just as *Sweeney Erect* is in part a dialogue with Shelley, and "Tradition and the Individual Talent" is in part a reply to Wordsworth. Although Eliot excludes his Romantic precursors from the tradition with which he defines his own work, he cannot, to use one of his favorite terms, "escape" them.

The transformations of *Sweeney Among the Nightingales* remain rather precarious: the carefully crafted quatrains can barely contain the poet's disgust with man's physical nature and his fear of grasping and animalistic women who threaten man at every turn. At the same time the poem exemplifies the struggles of one "individual talent" to come to terms with his own "tradition."

The poetry in *Ara Vos Prec* supports Eliot's suggestion in his first essay on Dante that "the contemplation of the horrid or sordid or disgusting, by an artist, is the necessary and negative aspect of the impulse toward the pursuit of beauty" (*SW*, 167). Like the scenes in the whip in the *Purgatorio*, these poems provide examples of misdirected love to be experienced by the reader (the *Vos* of the title) as a necessary stage in the purgatorial process. When the American edition of *Ara Vos Prec* appeared, however, it bore the simple title *Poems*. Eliot had clearly been trying to create a purgatorial framework for the collection by invoking the lines from Daniel, and the change in title may suggest his dissatisfaction with the results. Moments of violence and despair are carefully chronicled in *Ara Vos Prec*, but there is no promise of redemption and the tension between flesh and spirit, passions and intellect, remains largely unresolved.

Eliot's continuing fascination with the lines from *Purgatorio* 26 is evident in his next poem, *The Waste Land* (1922). Nowhere prior to *The Waste Land* had Eliot made such an abundant use of allusions and citations. Here they remain untranslated to emphasize their historicity and, in some cases, their quasi-sacred nature. In *The Waste Land*, Eliot explores further two issues that have become important for him: the uses a poet can make of his literary inheritance and the possibility a poet has of forming "new wholes" from varied experience. Dante is one of many authors whom Eliot cites in *The Waste Land*, but his significance far outweighs his actual presence. The example of Dante enables Eliot to create the purgatorial context he sought in *Ara Vos Prec*, a context that provides a way of evaluating the central experiences of the poem.

The citation from Daniel is by no means the only passage from the *Commedia* to inform *The Waste Land*, and critics have noted many parallels between Eliot's urban scene and Dante's *Inferno*.[13] Like the sufferers of Dante's *Inferno*, the characters of *The Waste Land* seem doomed to reenact their crimes continually. All the sins of lust in the seventh terrace—heterosexual and homosexual—are represented here, and those crimes which occur most frequently (Parts 2 and 3) result from misdirected or unfulfilled sexuality. Through the figure of Daniel, however, Eliot suggests a way of breaking out of the patterns of eternal repetition. At the conclusion of "The Fire Sermon," after presenting the reader with a series of sexual relationships, Eliot juxtaposes citations from St. Augustine, Zechariah, and the Buddha warning of the fires of lust. By establishing the fire imagery within a Dantean framework, Eliot is preparing for the possibility of purgation at the conclusion of the poem. Whereas Eliot had only presented examples of misdirected love in *Ara Vos Prec*, here he introduces an example of positive love as well. In this sense the work achieves in small measure the form of the *Purgatorio*, where illustrations of constructive love precede and balance illustrations of destructive love. In Dante's work, the reader confronts the positive before reexperiencing the negative.

Among the literary fragments that the speaker shores against his ruins at the end of The Waste Land is the concluding line of Purgatorio 26 ("Poi s'ascose nel foco che li affina") juxtaposed with a line from the Pervigilium Veneris ("Quando fiam uti chelidon").[14] Both citations suggest the productive change effected by purgatorial suffering as distinguished from the self-defeating suffering of the Inferno. In The Waste Land, however, this transformation remains largely a secular one. As late as 1927, Eliot was arguing that "Dante, qua poet, did not believe or disbelieve the Thomist cosmology or theory of the soul: he merely made use of it" (SE, 138), and the same could certainly be affirmed of Eliot's own use of Dante here. Following the example of Dante, Eliot asserts that fire need not only be destructive: it may be purgatorial as well, transforming lust into love and suffering into song.[15]

Following the publication of The Waste Land, Eliot, like the swallow, seemed to have lost his gift of song. Most of his energies were devoted to writing essays and reviews, editing the Criterion, and collecting his prose pieces for publication. His output of verse was slight. In this time of poetic drought, Eliot turned again to an intensive study of Dante, which resulted in "The Clark Lectures" given at Trinity College, Cambridge, in 1926, and later in Dante (1929). Through these extended analyses of Dante, Eliot laid the foundations for Ash Wednesday and Four Quartets.

"The Clark Lectures" are devoted to the metaphysical poets, but Eliot invokes Dante often in his discussions of "metaphysicality." According to a prefatory note, Eliot intended to expand the lectures into a book length study, The School of Donne, which was envisaged as part of a trilogy to be called "The Disintegration of the Intellect." Elizabethan Drama and The Sons of Ben were to be the other two volumes. The project was never executed, and "The Clark Lectures," which are absolutely central to an understanding of Eliot's mature view of Dante, remain unpublished, except for the first, which appeared in a French journal as "Deux attitudes mystiques: Dante et Donne."[16] That title suggests the importance of Dante to the lectures: indeed, he emerges as the metaphysical poet par excellence, and the example of Dante's "metaphysicality" provides Eliot with a means of resolving the poetic problems which confront him after *The Waste Land*.

In his first lecture, Eliot elaborates upon his earlier definition of "metaphysicality" as that power which poetry sometimes has to fuse "sense with thought." For Eliot, "metaphysical" becomes an evaluative term: "The metaphysical . . . gives the emotional equivalent of thought."[17] Eliot locates this characteristic in three historical periods: Italy in the trecento; Renaissance England; and nineteenth-century France, with Baudelaire and the symbolists. Most of the allusions in *The Waste Land* are from writers of these periods. As I have noted, Eliot places his own work in this tradition as well.

Eliot next distinguishes different ways by which thought can become poetry, a problem which was to concern him for the rest of his career. The first occurs when thought is "expressed in poetic form, though in the language of thought" (CL, 1:12). As an example, he quotes Edgar's words from Shakespeare's *King Lear* (V,ii): "Men must endure / Their going hence, even as their coming hither; / Ripeness is all." The second type he notes is "the discursive exposition of an argument," and he gives examples from *The Essay on Man*, "and at its highest, in the passages in the *Purgatorio* expounding the Thomist Aristotelian theory of the origin and development of the soul" (CL, 1:12). Eliot is aware of the difficulties of such verse: "Immense technical detail is necessary to make such discourse fly, and great emotional intensity is necessary to make it soar" (CL, 1:12). The third type, and the subject of "The Clark Lectures," is "that which occurs when an idea, or what is only ordinarily apprehensible as an intellectual statement, is translated in sensible form, so that the world of sense is actually enlarged" (CL, 1:12–13). It is precisely this to which Eliot aspires in his later poetry, and his attempts to define it here are extremely important:

> It becomes clear after a little inspection that this type of thought, the *Word Made Flesh* [Eliot circled and underlined these words], so to speak, is more restricted in the times and places of its avatar than is immediately evident. It is one form of an enlargement of immediate experience which, in one form or another, is a general function of poetry. . . . The characteristic of the type of poetry I am trying to

define is that it elevates sense for a moment to regions ordinarily
attainable only by abstract thought, or on the other hand clothes
the abstract, for a moment, with all the painful delight of flesh. [CL,
1:13–14]

Elsewhere in these lectures, Eliot calls this process incarnation, and his
choice of words points toward his own imminent religious conversion
and his concern with "the word" in Ash Wednesday. This process is also
akin to the transformation described by Dante in the Purgatorio, a transformation which heretofore Eliot has employed in a secular sense. Before
turning to Ash Wednesday, where these distinctions become crucial, we
should consider Eliot's short book, Dante.

Dante appeared as a volume in "The Poets on the Poets" series published by Faber and Faber. It is an introductory work intended for the
general reader and therefore far less speculative than "The Clark Lectures." In a note to chapter 2, however, Eliot raises the question of beliefs
in poetry. Having quoted one of his favorite lines from Dante, "E'n la sua
volontade è nostra pace" ("In His will is our peace") (Paradiso 3.85), Eliot
declares that "the statement of Dante seems to me literally true. And I
confess that it has more beauty for me now, when my own experience
has deepened its meaning, than it did when I first read it. So I can only
conclude that I cannot, in practice, wholly separate my poetic appreciation from my personal beliefs" (Dante, 59). This represents a radical shift
from his earlier position quoted above. His declaration suggests that the
influence of Dante will be considerably more pervasive than in the past.

Throughout Dante, Eliot adumbrates the qualities of Dante's work he
most admires and then considers those scenes that are for him the high
points of the Commedia. The only passage "at all comparable to those of
the Inferno" (Dante, 39) is, not surprisingly, Dante's meeting with Daniel in
Canto 26 of the Purgatorio. Eliot's discussion of this canto is sufficiently
important to warrant quotation in full:

> In this canto the Lustful are purged in flame, yet we see clearly how
> the flame of purgatory differs from that of hell. In hell, the torment
> issues from the very nature of the damned themselves, expresses
> their essence; they writhe in the torment of their own perpetually
> perverted nature. In purgatory the torment of flame is deliberately

and consciously accepted by the penitent. When Dante approaches with Virgil these souls in purgatory flame, they crowd towards him:

Poi verso me, quanto potevan farsi,
     certi si feron, sempre con riguardo
     di non uscir dove non fossero arsi.

Then certain of them made towards me, so far as they could, but ever watchful not to come so far that they should not be in the fire.

The souls in purgatory suffer because they wish to suffer, for purgation. And observe that they suffer more actively and keenly, being souls preparing for blessedness, than Virgil suffers in eternal limbo. In their suffering is hope, in the anaesthesia of Virgil is hopelessness; that is the difference. The canto ends with the superb verses of Arnaut Daniel in his Provençal tongue. [Dante, 39–40]

Unlike his friend Pound, Eliot is concerned with Dante's depiction of Daniel's experience rather than with Daniel's art, and he employs the experience to distinguish between suffering in the Purgatorio and the Inferno. In the Purgatorio, suffering is willful and leads to a transcendence of the sin: for Daniel, eros is transformed into agape. This doctrine provides a way of evaluating the experience of The Waste Land, although in a secular sense, and it becomes even more central to Eliot's next major poem, Ash Wednesday.

Ash Wednesday was written at a turning point in Eliot's life, "nel mezzo del cammin" (he was forty-two when it was published in final form). It was his most Dantean poem to date: although cast in the form of a penitential prayer, Eliot combines elements from the Inferno to suggest the importance of the poem's occurring at a moment of personal crisis for the speaker. We are continually reminded of the opening of Dante's poem; in the three leopards of Part 2, for example, recalling the lion, the leopard, and the she-wolf Dante confronts, and in the remembrance of "eternal dolour" (Part 4), evoking the inscription above the entrance to the Inferno. The speaker is suffering a personal hell: he is plagued by sensual desires and self-doubt, and he acknowledges the need to renounce the things of this world as a state in his conversion. His spiritual and sensual crises are closely related. Throughout *Ara Vos Prec*, Eliot employed religious terminology for sacred and profane problems, but the issues remained fragmented in that volume. Now, the example of Dante and the poets of the *stil nuovo* "to enlarge the boundary of human love so as to make it a stage in the progress toward the divine" suggests a way of resolving this dilemma (CL, 6:6). In *Ash Wednesday*, Eliot recognizes the necessity of having an intermediary, a woman modeled in many ways after Dante's Beatrice, who can aid in the transformation of sensual love into sacred love. Francis Fergusson has noted "Dante's lifelong habit of taking a loved woman, at every significant juncture of his life, as the objectively visible pattern of the spirit's movement,"[18] and Eliot is following him here. This attempt "to enlarge the boundary of human love" is reflected not only in Eliot's development of an intermediary, but also in his use of allusions. The first line of the poem, for example, is a translation of the opening line of Cavalcanti's *ballettetta*, "Perch'io non spero di tornar giammai." Fearing the imminence of death and feeling the despair of exile, Cavalcanti confesses to his lady that he never expects to return to her. Eliot translates the line, conceals his source, and employs it in a radically different way: he expands its meaning (hence the translation of "turn" [tornar] rather than "return") by transposing it from a profane to a sacred context. His citation from Shakespeare (1.4) illustrates the same process. These alterations exemplify the transformations of the secular into the sacred which is a central theme of the poem.

In the concluding lines of *The Waste Land*, Eliot presented "fragments" that affirmed, among other things, the power of the artist to transform personal suffering into a work of beauty. Eliot discussed this problem in "Shakespeare and the Stoicism of Seneca" (1927), citing first Dante and then Shakespeare as a poet who "was occupied with the struggle—which alone constitutes life for a poet—to transmute his personal and private agonies into something rich and strange, something universal and impersonal" (SE, 137). *Ash Wednesday* is a poem that speaks to the fears of an artist who may have lost his power to create, and it finally renews the affirmation of *The Waste Land*, but in a greatly altered context. Eliot now sees the transforming power of art as a demonstration of God's power. When Eliot characterizes metaphysical poetry (and especially the poetry of Dante) as the *Word Made Flesh*, he is illuminating the religious drama of incarnation as well as the poetic process of creativity. In *Ash Wednesday*,

Eliot sees the relationship as more than a mere analogy. His own creativity becomes an affirmation of the process of incarnation.

Nearly all of the allusions of Ash Wednesday are concealed, and this signals a definitive change in Eliot's poetic practice.[19] The singular exception is the utterance "Sovegna vos" (Part 4), which remains untranslated partly as a tribute to Daniel, partly for its auditory value, but largely to locate the plight of the protagonist. Ash Wednesday deals with the speaker's ascension of the purgatorial mountain and his struggles with the sensual and worldly temptations of which he knows he must purge himself. He asks the lady (and, as always, the reader) to remember his plight, with the hope that he is worthy of "refinement" and can transcend his suffering. In the Purgatorio, Dante passes through the flames and is greeted by Beatrice, who has him reappraise his past life before his transformation can be completed. This step is not taken in Ash Wednesday, but the success of the poem as a work of art provides a partial testimony to a central issue of the work (the speaker's lack of faith in his creativity), and this in turn affirms his faith in the powers of a deity whose own power his artistic abilities dimly mirror.

Clearly it is a Christian Eliot invoking a Christian Dante in Ash Wednesday; the question of transformation, so important to Eliot's work, at last becomes a religious one. Although the fire and the rose are yet to be one, a movement toward unification is begun here, made possible for Eliot by the perspective gained from his study of Dante.

In Four Quartets, Eliot reconsiders these issues in a more universal context. Again, it is the example of Dante that permits him to achieve a satisfying resolution. This occurs in Little Gidding, where Eliot combines citation with imitation to produce his most sustained homage to Dante. Eliot has commented on the difficulties of producing an English equivalent of terza rima (Critic, 128–29); the lines are an extraordinary tour de force, revealing how markedly his sensibility was affected by Dante.

Both the season (winter) and the dominant element (fire) of Little Gidding are predetermined by the pattern of Four Quartets, but Eliot develops each in a Dantean manner. The poem opens with the "sempiternal" season, the adjective echoing "di quelle sempiterne rose" of Dante's Paradiso (12.19). This is the season of the pentecostal fires and these two forces work against each other until, at the conclusion of Part 5, a unification of fire and rose is achieved. But Eliot does not explicitly characterize the fire in Part 2 as "refining fire" in the early drafts. In a prose description which preceded composition of the passage, Eliot noted:

> Winter scene. May.
> Lyric. air earth water end & &
> daemonic fire. The Inferno.
>   They vanish, the individuals, and
> our feeling for them sinks into the
> flame which refines. They emerge
> in another pattern & recreated & reconciled
> redeemed, having their meaning to-
> gether not apart, in a union
> which is of beams from the central
> fire. And the others with them
> contemporaneous.
> Invocation to the Holy Spirit.[20]

However, the only lines in the Magdalene College draft alluding to purga-torial flames are three which follow the section on the "death of water and fire," and here the connection remains vague:

> Fire without and fire within
> Expel/Purge the unidentified sin
> This is the place where we begin.   [Quartets, 168]

   Other allusions to Dante are much more explicit in this draft, but, like the fire, they are drawn largely from the Inferno. The ghost so central to the passage in imitation of terza rima is not a "familiar compound ghost," but rather a "vague familiar ghost," and he is identified directly: "Are you here, Ser Brunetto?" Eliot greatly admired all of the important recogni-tion scenes of the Commedia, and this one in particular he has spoken of at length (Dante, 28–29; CL, 4:4–5). It is significant that this confrontation occurs at a point where Eliot is seeking to reconcile time and eternity. As Dante acknowledges in the Inferno, it was Brunetto who taught him how man makes himself eternal ("come l'uom s'etterna" [15.85]) by absorbing the traditions of the past and revitalizing them in the present, and this had been one of the lessons of "Tradition and the Individual Talent." But in spite of Brunetto's reputation as a teacher and writer, his remarks to the speaker in the early drafts of Little Gidding neglect the craft of verse entirely. Instead there is a longing for the past quite absent in the final version:

Remember . . .
   The wild strawberries eaten in the garden,
   The walls of Poitiers, and the Anjou wine,
The fresh new season's rope, the smell of varnish
   On the clean oar, the drying of the sails,
Such things as seem of least and most importance.
So, as you circumscribe this dreary round,
   Shall your life pass from you, with all you hated
   And all you loved, the future and the past.
United to another past, another future,
   (After many seas and after many lands)
   The dead and the unborn, who shall be nearer
Than the voices and the faces that were most near.   [Quartets, 183]

Eliot concludes this section on a note of peaceful acceptance:

   This is the final gift of earth accorded
   One soil, one past, one future, in one place.
Nor shall the eternal thereby be remoter
   But nearer: seek or seek not, it is here.
   Now, the last love on earth. The rest is grace.   [Quartets, 183.4]

Here, as in the earlier *Ode*, the materials seem excessively personal, recalling, perhaps, Eliot's travels with Pound in the South of France and his youthful experiences sailing off the coast of Massachusetts. But in the revisions Eliot replaced Brunetto Latini with the "familiar compound ghost" who embodies the speaker's poetic forebears. This "ghost" incorporates a tradition stretching from Dante to Yeats and can address a much broader range of problems—poetic and personal, past, present, and future—than could Latini. His speech becomes a moment of transition in the poem by reintroducing the image of fire, and by making it explicitly purgatorial:

From wrong to wrong the exasperated spirit
   Proceeds, unless restored by that refining fire
   Where you must move in measure, like a dancer.

In a letter to John Hayward (27 August 1942), Eliot spoke of this change:

> I think you will recognise that it was necessary to get rid of Bru-
> netto for two reasons. The first is that the visionary figure has now
> become somewhat more definite and will no doubt be identified
> by some readers with Yeats though I do not mean anything so pre-
> cise as that. However, I do not wish to take the responsibility of
> putting Yeats or anybody else into Hell and I do not want to impute
> to him the particular vice which took Brunetto there. Secondly,
> although the reference to that Canto is intended to be explicit, I
> wished the effect of the whole to be Purgatorial, which is much
> more appropriate. That brings us to the reference to swimming in
> fire which you will remember at the end of Purgatorio 26 where
> the poets are found. The active co-operation is, I think, sound the-
> ology and is certainly sound Dante, because the people who talk to
> him at that point are represented as not wanting to waste time in
> conversation but wishing to dive back into the fire to accomplish
> their expiation. [Quartets, 65–66]

As Eliot notes in this letter, the suffering in Purgatory is actively sought
because it leads to atonement. By making the fires of Little Gidding purgatorial rather than infernal, he affirms one of the lessons of The Waste Land:
suffering can be productive for an artist who is able to transform that
suffering into a work of art. Here, infused by Eliot's Christian beliefs, the
"refining fires" make possible a "restoration" that results in a "metaphysical" reconciliation of passion and thought, thus going beyond the secular
assertion of The Waste Land. But before making such an affirmation, Eliot
reasserts the dual nature of fire and, as a corollary, the dual nature of
love:

> The dove descending breaks the air
> With flame of incandescent terror
> Of which the tongues declare
> The one discharge from sin and error.
> The only hope, or else despair
>   Lies in the choice of pyre or pyre—
>   To be redeemed from fire by fire.

Who then devised the torment? Love.
Love is the unfamiliar Name
Behind the hands that wove
The intolerable shirt of flame
Which human power cannot remove.
We only live, only suspire
Consumed by either fire or fire.

Passage through the refining fire is the final stage in the transformation of love in the *Purgatorio*. Only after the completion of this process can a new life begin in which "the fire and the rose are one." Eliot takes a significant step beyond *Ash Wednesday* here. With the example of Dante, he is finally able to achieve a metaphysical union of sense and thought. In retrospect, it would appear that all of Eliot's poetry had been moving toward this moment of reconciliation.

With the opening line of *The Love Song of J. Alfred Prufrock*, Eliot invites the reader to accompany him on a journey whose end is only reached in the final lines of *Little Gidding*. Dante was Eliot's Virgil, and as Eliot came to understand his guide, he understood himself. At crucial moments in his career, the example of Dante enabled him to extend his work in significant new directions. In addition, Dante's work formed the cornerstone of a poetic tradition created by Eliot, a tradition which enabled him to liberate himself from the shadow of his precursors. The passage from Canto 26 of the *Purgatorio* provided him with a means of resolving the central issues—both poetic and personal—that confronted him, and it is a paradigm of his use of Dante. For Eliot, Dante was the first complete metaphysical poet, fusing the realms of sense and thought: he himself strove to be the latest.

NOTES

1. T. S. Eliot, *To Criticize the Critic* (London: Faber and Faber, 1965), p. 125. Hereafter referred to as *Critic*.

2. Charles S. Singelton, ed. and trans., *Dante Alighieri, The Divine Comedy: Purgatorio* (Princeton: Princeton University Press, Bollingen Series, 1970), p. 288. All subse-

quent citations and translations are from this edition. References are to canto and line number.

3. T. S. Eliot, *Dante* (London: Faber and Faber, 1929), pp. 12–13. Hereafter referred to as *D*.

4. C. H. Grandgent, ed., *Dante Alighieri, La Divina Commedia* (Cambridge: Harvard University Press, 1972), p. 542. This edition was first published in 1909.

5. Ezra Pound, *The Spirit of Romance* (Norfolk, Conn.: New Directions, n.d.), p. 21. Hereafter referred to as *Romance*.

6. Eliot apparently used this text for *The Waste Land* as well, for the same textual errors are duplicated there.

7. Mario Praz, *The Flaming Heart* (New York: W. W. Norton, 1973), p. 350.

8. T. S. Eliot, *The Sacred Wood* (London: Methuen & Co., 1969), p. 167. Hereafter referred to as *SW*.

9. This is a phrase Eliot uses in "The Metaphysical Poets," reprinted in T. S. Eliot, *Selected Essays* (New York: Harcourt, Brace, 1950), p. 248. Hereafter referred to as *SE*.

10. Eliot, "Hamlet and his Problems," *SE*, p. 123.

11. Remy de Gourmont, *Promenades Littéraires* (Paris: Mercure de France, 1904), p. 106.

12. F. O. Matthiessen, *The Achievement of T. S. Eliot* (New York: Oxford University Press, 1959), p. 129.

13. See, for example, Philip R. Headings, *T. S. Eliot* (New York: Twayne Publishers, 1964), p. 57.

14. One remembers the juxtaposition of the *Pervigilium Veneris* and Arnaut Daniel in *The Spirit of Romance*.

15. This is not the only place in *The Waste Land* in which Eliot alludes to this passage, although it is the most important. For his dedication, Eliot transfers Guinizelli's tribute ("il miglior fabbro") from Arnaut Daniel to Ezra Pound. Given Daniel's importance for Eliot, this dedication assumes a significance it would not otherwise have. Like Statius's praise of Virgil (Canto 21), Guinizelli's lines acknowledge the authority of a greater poet, and this is a type of recognition Eliot cherished. In *The Waste Land: A Facsimile and Transcript*, there is a third use of these lines. Eliot experimented with two different lines from this passage as possible conclusions to the poem *Exequy*. Although, on the advice of Pound, Eliot dropped all of the short poems, Daniel's presence here is one more testament to the obsessive appeal of this passage on his imagination.

16. "Deux attitudes mystiques: Dante et Donne," *Chroniques*, Paris, 3 (1927): 149–73.

17. T. S. Eliot, "The Clark Lectures," 1:7–8. Unpublished MS at King's College, Cambridge University. Hereafter referred to as *CL*.

18. Francis Fergusson, *Dante* (New York: Macmillan, 1966), p. 197.

19. This was not the case when the sections of the poem were first published. The line from Cavalcanti, for example, formed the title to the first section. See Grover Smith, *T. S. Eliot's Poetry and Plays: A Study in Sources and Meaning* (Chicago and London: The University of Chicago Press, 1956), pp. 130–59, for a discussion of the sources.

20. Helen Gardner, *The Composition of Four Quartets* (New York: Oxford University Press, 1978), p. 157.

MONROE K. SPEARS

The Divine Comedy of W. H. Auden

To couple any modern poet's work with Dante's is to risk suggesting the comic incongruity of such titles as *The Hamlet of A. MacLeish* or *Sweeney Agonistes*. Yet my title is, I believe, justifiable. Dante called his poem a comedy, he said in his letter to Can Grande, because it ends happily and its language is "lax and humble . . . the vernacular speech in which very women communicate."[1] Since the mythological Poet of Auden's later work certainly regards his own fate as a happy one, and since one of his stylistic triumphs was the perfecting of a diction at once personal and various, Auden's poems may be described as a comedy according to Dante's criteria. Unlike Dante's or such later grim comedies as Balzac's *Comédie humaine* or *Pagliacci* ("La commedia è finita!"), Auden's poems are also frequently comic in the modern sense of being funny.

The epithet *divine* that Boccaccio attached to Dante's title is harder to justify in Auden's case. Unfortunately, it is no longer possible to bestow with a straight face such an honorific upon any modern poet. As simple description, however, it indicates accurately that Auden's work is concerned with the divine—though with the divine as it appears in this world rather than with the divine other worlds of Dante. Auden argues, in fact, that comedy is the only mode in which the divine can be represented in human affairs. Falstaff is "a comic symbol for the supernatural order of Charity as contrasted with the temporal order of Justice"; his "untiring devotion to making others laugh becomes a comic image for a love which is absolutely self-giving"; Bertie Wooster, guided by Jeeves, is the Christian counterpart of the Quest hero: "So speaks comically—and in what other mode than the comic could it on earth truthfully speak?—the voice of Agape, of Holy Love."[2]

In his own career, Auden brought together the comic and the divine. The pleasure in clowning, farce, and elaborate jokes and games that co-exists uneasily in his early works with the sense of doom, the ominous foreboding, and the strong satirical impulse is justified and set free by his acceptance of that ultimate Absurdity and foolishness to the world, Christianity. In the Christian view, as Simeon puts it in For the Time Being, "The tragic conflict of Virtue with Necessity is no longer confined to the Exceptional Hero. . . . Every invalid is Roland . . . every stenographer Brünnhilde. . . . Nor is the Ridiculous a species any longer of the Ugly; for since of themselves all men are without merit, all are ironically as-sisted to their comic bewilderment by the Grace of God."[3] There is no longer any distinction between trivial and serious situations: "Every tea-table is a battlefield . . . every martyrdom an occasion for flip cracks and sententious oratory" (CP, 300). As one might expect, once these defini-tions have been made, examples of divine comedy abound in Auden's work. But let us look somewhat more closely at the shape of his career.

One way of juxtaposing Auden and Dante is to consider Auden's oeu-vre as falling into three stages corresponding to the three realms of the Commedia. The early poems (through 1939) constitute an Inferno, in which the inhabitants of "this country of ours where nobody is well"[4] reveal their spiritual faults through physical appearance and posture. As in Dante, the sinners are in Hell because they refuse to change; they are "Holders of one position, wrong for years," and their attitudes and activi-ties are emblematic of their sins. "Stork-legged heaven-reachers," "com-pulsory touchers," those who are "prey to fugues"—all these are ill be-cause they are wicked; but wickedness is defined as obedience to the Devil of conscious control. Auden's earliest versions of this doctrine are somewhat peculiar because he picked it up in Berlin from "loony La-yard," who got it mainly from the American healer Homer Lane; he soon shows acquaintance, however, with its great renderings in Blake, Law-rence, Groddeck, and Freud. In this transvaluation of values, the existing society and the education that supports it are seen as evil. Repression and guilt create our enemies. But our enemies, since they oppose the present society and the psychological and moral distortions upon which it is based, are really our friends. Hence the title Auden gives in 1945 to the most famous ode from *The Orators* is *Which Side Am I Supposed To Be On?* The cure, in brief, is "To throw away the key and walk away," to reject the well-meaning advice of the elders (*Have a Good Time*), not to follow *The Decoys* but to go "out of this house" and migrate (geographically or chronologically, transferring allegiance to the future). But it is not simple; this is no Hell for others only, and "our" feelings are profoundly mixed.

In 1932 Auden began a long poem that he never finished or published,[5] an epic modeled on the *Divine Comedy* in verse based on *Piers Plowman*. Like Dante's and Langland's, it is a dream-vision; but the tone is mock-epic, sometimes suggesting Pope's *Rape of the Lock*. (The first line is, "In the year of my youth when yoyos came in.") In narrative and dramatic structure, it follows Dante closely; but its Virgil-figure resembles his friend, Gerald Heard. Perhaps because of the inadequacy of his guidance through modern life, among other problems, Auden seems to have abandoned the poem in 1933.

Address for a Prize-Day[6] in *The Orators* (1932) translates Dante's analysis of love in the *Purgatorio* into burlesque psychosomatic terms and reduces it to the level of schoolboy pep talks and moral exhortations. Excessive lovers of self suffer from "cataract or deafness"; "excessive lovers of their neighbors" are "dare-devils of the soul," secretly passionate, heavy smokers; defective lovers are "anaemic, muscularly undeveloped and rather mean," full of inertia and unacted desires. Perverted lovers may be detected by "a slight proneness to influenza, perhaps, a fear of cows. . . . Is he one? Was she one?" (*TEA*, 62–63). In *The Dog Beneath the Skin* (1935)[7] there is a parody sermon, *Depravity*, that operates similarly: the simple-minded Vicar puts absurdly and distortedly what nevertheless has a germ of truth. Thus he describes the war in heaven, with the defeat of the rebel angels: "Into the fosse of Hell they fell like water. Hurrah! Hurrah! Hurrah!" Then "the world became an everlasting invalid," and God "a very merciful and loving physician." But his "enemies have launched another offensive, on the grandest scale, . . . under the same deluding banner of Freedom" (*Dog*, 147–48), and the Vicar concludes with patriotic fervor. Another scene in the same play describes a hospital in psychosomatic terms: "See passion transformed into rheumatism; rebellion into paralysis; power into a tumour.... For those who reject their gifts: choose here their punishment" (*Dog*, 91). The final chorus draws the moral: "Mourn not for these; these are ghosts who chose their pain, / Mourn rather for yourselves; and your inability to make up your minds / ... Choose therefore that you may recover" (*Dog*, 160). *Petition*, a parody of petitionary prayer (but, like those we have been discussing, not merely a parody), represents God as a divine psychiatrist or healer: "Sir, no man's enemy, forgiving all / But will his negative inversion ... / Prohibit sharply the rehearsed response / And gradually correct the coward's stance."

While Auden in this first period thus shows some influence of Dante in imagery and in modes of thought, and while this whole stage of his work may be considered as a generalized parallel to the *Inferno*, his explicit references to Dante suggest that Auden at this time regarded him as associated with the past and with established and conventional religion, and hence of limited relevance. For example, the reference in the dedication of *The Ascent of F 6* (1936) to the "stricken grove" of suicides (*Inferno* 13) is evidence that Dante was on Auden's mind, as is the opening scene of the play, in which Ransom reads the Ulysses passage from *Inferno* 26 and interprets Dante in Freudian terms as vengeful and power hungry. In the verse *Commentary* to *In Time of War* (1938) he views as irrevocably past the united Europe in which "the flint-faced exile wrote his three-act comedy" (*TEA*, 268).

In his second stage, however, Auden feels Dante to be highly relevant. As he reexamines his beliefs in the shadow of approaching war and moves toward a new religious commitment, he invokes Dante's presence. Beginning in 1939, he engages in a strenuous rethinking of ideas, self-examination, and reformulation of attitudes that may be called purgatorial. This activity results, from 1940 to 1947, in the most ambitious long poems of Auden's career. He takes Dante explicitly as guide in the first of these and ends the period with an allegorical dream-vision in which the characters seek to recover Eden.

The poem *They* on its first appearance in September 1939[8] (when it was called *Crisis*) had an epigraph from *Purgatorio* 14.85–87: "Of my sowing such straw I reap. O human folk, why set the heart there where exclusion of partnership is necessary?"[9] The speaker in Dante, Guido del Duca, is describing the sin of Envy, from which he is being purged. Auden's poem is a psychological interpretation of the beginning of World War II. Asking "Where do They come from? Those whom we so much dread," it answers that "We have conjured them here like a lying map; / ... the crooked that dreads to be straight / Cannot alter its prayer but summons / Out of the dark a horrible rector" (CP, 202). Thus the enemy is self-created, the result of our spiritual failures, our "exclusion of partnership."

Freud, in the elegy published in January 1940, is praised for his Dantean compassion; the parallel between neurotics and the damned is made explicit; and the Freudian Eros is praised as against the denials of conventional religion: "Of course they called on God; but he went his way, / Down among the Lost People like Dante, down / To the stinking fosse where the injured / Lead the ugly life of the rejected. / And showed us what evil is, not, as we thought, / deeds that must be punished, but our lack of faith ..." (CP, 216). Over his grave "Sad is Eros, builder of cities, / And weeping anarchic Aphrodite" (CP, 216). This poem expresses the "transvaluation of values" we have seen in the early verse; but the position is not difficult to reconcile with the existential Christianity Auden soon came to accept. In both, the "courage to be"—to use the phrase Paul Tillich later made famous—is the essence of faith.[10]

The transition is reflected in New Year Letter, dated 1 January 1940. Here Auden chooses Dante as his judge-confessor in the imaginary tribunal all writers must face: "That lean hard-bitten pioneer" who was "By Amor Rationalis led / Through the three kingdoms of the dead" (CP, 164). Dante's respectability is mitigated by his companions, "self-educated WILLIAM BLAKE" and "the adolescent with red hands," Rimbaud; but Dante is the master chosen above all others. (In a prose essay published the next year Auden identified Dante, Langland, and Pope as the three greatest influences on his poetry.)[11]

Dante is a constant presence in New Year Letter. At the beginning Auden, in describing the city crowd, sees the Dantean allusion through Eliot's eyes, as Eliot saw it through Baudelaire's: "Along the streets the people flow / Singing or sighing as they go" (CP, 161). Part 2 begins with a description of "strangers, enemies, and friends" lost in darkness on the Mountain: "And intense in the mountain frost / The heavy breathing of the lost; / Far down below them whence they came / Still flickers feebly a red flame, / A tiny glow in the great void / Where an existence was destroyed" (CP, 167).

The heart of the poem is its interpretation of the *Commedia*, and especially the *Purgatorio*, in psychological terms. We cannot will Heaven but are free to negate our wills in Hell; Hell is, in fact, the "being of the lie / That we become if we deny / The laws of consciousness" and its fire "the pain to which we go / If we refuse to suffer. . . ." Thus our only positive choice is Purgatory: willing ourselves to it, we are "Consenting parties to our lives" (CP, 178).

This is to accept the world of Time: "In Time we sin. / But Time is sin and can forgive; / Time is the life with which we live / At least three quarters of our time, / The purgatorial hill we climb" (CP, 178). Such mountaineering is "the only game / At which we show a natural skill," so "We have no cause to look dejected / When, wakened from a dream of glory, / We find ourselves in Purgatory, / Back on the same old mountain side / With only guessing for a guide" (CP, 179). We are, in fact, relieved to find ourselves back on "its damp earth" where we have always lived: "Its inconveniences are known, / And we have made its flaws our own. / Is it not here that we belong, / Where everyone is doing wrong, / And normal our freemartin state, / Half angel and half *petite bête*?" (CP, 179). So the poet urges that we set out again, "perched upon the sharp arête, / When if we do not move we fall, / Yet movement is heretical, / . . . Admitting every step we make / Will certainly be a mistake, / But still believing we can climb / A little higher every time" (CP, 179). Through this purgatory of daily life "No route is truly orthodox" and our faith is "well balanced by our doubt," requiring a "reverent frivolity"; but though far from a literal equivalent of Dante's Purgatory, it is still essentially the same: "the penitential way / That forces our wills to be free" (CP, 179).

With his gift for plunging straight to essentials, Auden keeps steadily in view what he takes to be the central doctrine of the *Commedia*, as it is its literal center. This is the exposition in Cantos 14–19 of the *Purgatorio* of Love as motive force of both good and bad in us, and as going astray through being perverted, defective, or excessive. (We have already seen this distorted in *Address for a Prize-Day*; the Vicar in *The Dog Beneath the Skin* calls it "the positive tropism of the soul to God.") The structure of Purgatory—the topography of its Mountain—embodies this doctrine: the sins of perverted Love are worst because they destroy our relation to God and our neighbors or prevent us from loving our neighbors as ourselves; and these sins—Pride, Envy, Anger—are dealt with on the lowest terraces of the mountain. It is typical of Auden's quick, no-nonsense practicality that he should fix his attention not on the picturesque horrors of Hell but on the most practical part of the most human division of the Comedy—these lower terraces where the work begins of purging the major sins, so that one can then get on with the task of climbing the mountain.

The two passages in Dante that Auden cites most often are both quoted in the notes to *New Year Letter*. The first is Virgil's discourse on love: "Nor creator nor creature, my son, was ever without love, either natural or rational; and this thou knowest. The natural is always without error; but the other may err through an evil object, or through too little or too much vigour. . . . Hence thou mayst understand that love must be the seed of every virtue in you, and of every deed that deserves punishment" (*Purgatorio* 17.91–105). The second contrasts Charity to Envy: "the more people on high who comprehend each other, the more there are to love well, and the more love is there, and, like a mirror, one giveth back to the other" (*Purgatorio* 15.73–75).[12] In his earlier verse, Auden had sometimes opposed the "pure in heart" to the wicked and neurotic, but at other times held that nobody is pure in heart, because Eros is selfish and tends toward evil; it must therefore be distinguished sharply from Agape, selfless Christian love that comes only through Grace, when Auden approaches Christian belief once more. In *New Year Letter* he notes that the task prescribed by both Eros and Apollo is "to set in order" (and quotes in the notes the famous prayer of Jacopone da Todi: "O Thou who lovest me, set my love in order"). But, though he posits a reconciliation of Eros and Agape through Logos (the Word or the Law), the solution is not very convincing: "We need to love all since we are / Each a unique particular / . . . We can love each because we know / All, all of us, that this is so" (CP, 192). In the next few years Auden shifts from this initial tendency to regard Eros and Agape as wholly distinct (in the manner of Kierkegaard, Barth, Nygren, and extreme Protestants in general) to the view that they are conjoinable in the Catholic concept of *Caritas*.[13] This trend away from Gnostic or Manichean tendencies is very much in the spirit of Dante.

The setting in order required by Eros, Apollo, and Agape is accomplished especially in the long poems For the Time Being and The Sea and the Mirror; but naturally enough, Dante has no place in either the Christmas oratorio or the Shakespearean closet-drama, except in the occasional image: "Descend into the fosse of Tribulation, / Take the cold hand of Terror for a guide; / Below you in its swirling desolation / Hear tortured Horror roaring for a bride" so that you may "wake, a child in the rose-garden" (CP, 286). The last of the long poems, however, The Age of Anxiety, is in some respects an explicit parallel or contrast to Dante's poem, since it is a quest, a dream-vision, and in part an allegory. The time is the night of All Souls, and the characters are, metaphorically, souls in Purgatory, each dreaming in his own way of escape. There is a generalized parallel with the Purgatorio in the sevenfold division of ages and stages and in the vision of innocence as goal. But the visions of Auden's characters are alcoholically induced, their quests are entirely subjective, consisting of fantasy and regression, and the innocence they seek is the lost Eden of childhood. The poem is a sympathetic satire on the attempts of these representative moderns to escape anxiety and guilt through their own efforts. The community that they briefly and precariously achieve is a pathetic semblance of that felt by Dante as he proceeds up the Mountain to Eden, where Love and Law are one. None of Auden's characters has any intimation of the possibility of faith, except for Malin who, at the very end, makes explicit the "negative knowledge" that is all the poem offers.

The respects in which The Age of Anxiety most invites comparison with The Divine Comedy are—perhaps inevitably—those in which it has been most criticized. For example, the "carrying meter," the flexible alliterative line without rhyme. Randall Jarrell dismissed Auden's use of it with withering contempt as monotonous and trivial, but Robert Lowell more recently described it as a "masterpiece of metrics" and commented on its perpetual fascination as such, whatever its other limitations.[14] In "The Seven Stages," Auden's one attempt at extended and systematic allegory, there is, as far as I can see, no explicit resemblance to Dante: the mode of imagery, based on equivalence between landscape and other topographical features and the anatomy of the human body, is quite different. But the distortions of Eros (the dean making "bedroom eyes at a beefsteak," the surrealist voyage to Venus Island) and the pursuit of false Edens are based on Dantean concepts and are among the best parts of the poem. It is in the sixth of the Seven Ages that man "pines for some / Nameless Eden where he never was / But where in his wishes once again / . . . the children play" (CP, 366). In the Seven Stages, the characters succeed in their regressive goal of recovering (in their communal alcoholic vision) the Eden of lost childhood innocence; but the "extraordinary charm of these gardens . . . seems an accusation. They become uneasy and unwell," each aware of his own lack of goodness. Later, as they celebrate the courtship of Rosetta and Emble, they share once more a vision of Eden, but this time in the future: "Alcohol, lust, fatigue, and the longing to be good, had by now induced in them all a euphoric state in which it seemed as if it were only some trifling and easily rectifiable error . . . which was keeping mankind from the millennial Earthly Paradise" (CP, 399). But instead, even the courtship falls through, and Rosetta gives up her fantasies to come to terms with her true childhood, as, to varying degrees, do the other characters. The comparison to Dante leaves something to be said for Auden, here as elsewhere.

In Auden's third stage, consisting of the poems written since 1947, there is an emphasis on apprehension of the Sacred and the celebration of Joy, communal as well as individual, that suggests a parallel to the *Paradiso*. As to Joy, Auden moves from a paradoxical obedience of the "absurd command—Rejoice" (CP, 248) to a broader definition of "That singular command / I do not understand / *Bless what there is for being,* / Which has to be obeyed" (CP, 450) to the simple conviction that we are "created to love and be happy." Defining poetry as a verbal rite of homage to sacred objects or beings, he says that it must "praise all it can for being as for happening" and suggests that all things are potentially sacred, though each individual recognizes only a limited number as such. *Homage to Clio* (1960) embodies this doctrine of poetry as acceptance and celebration, with one of its principal functions the "preservation and renewal of natural piety toward every kind of created excellence" in human or external nature. In prose, he makes explicit the development of his attitude from its original existentialist (and specifically Kierkegaardian) cast to a more catholic one. Thus he writes in 1952, expounding Kierkegaard, that the paradoxical position of suffering is well expressed by the penitent shade of Forese when he says to Dante, "And not once only, while circling this road, is our pain renewed: I say pain and ought to say solace" (*Purgatorio* 23.70–73). But in his later (1968) essay on Kierkegaard, he stresses the peculiarities arising both from the nature of Protestantism and from his personal limitations. Kierkegaard, he says, was in his sensibility a Manichee. The Passion was to his taste; the Nativity and Epiphany were not. In contrast, Auden quotes Bonhoeffer: "We should love God eternally with our whole hearts, yet not so as to compromise or diminish our earthly affections. . . . If He pleases to grant us some overwhelming earthly bliss, we ought not to try and be more religious than God himself."[15]

Auden's increasing concern with community in the later poetry is summed up thus in 1960:

> The Christian doctrine which Protestantism emphasizes is that every human being . . . is unique before God; the complementary and equally Christian doctrine emphasized by Catholicism is that we are all members . . . both in the Earthly and the Heavenly City . . . Whether one considers oneself, one's friends and neighbors, or the history of the last hundred years, it seems clear that the principal threat to a sense of identity is our current lack of belief in and acceptance of the existence of others [Forewords, 87].

In the poetry the communal sense becomes more and more clearly expressed in terms of time. Thus at the end of For the Time Being the time is noon, which for Auden means the undramatic and drab present: "the time is noon: / When the Spirit must practice his scales of rejoicing / Without even a hostile audience" (CP, 308). Nones and the volume of which it is the title poem (1951) develop this symbol: the poem is set in the siesta hour (3:00 P.M.) of sleepy stillness, after the act but before the consequences; the Crucifixion, the archetypal sin, has taken place, and we, the crowd, "are left alone with our feat." Now we can no longer believe ourselves innocent; we see that evil must have its sway; and it is as well, temporarily, for our minds to try to escape. (Consider in contrast Dante's statement in the Convito that "The hour of noon is the noblest in the whole day and the one of greatest virtue" since it is the hour of Christ's death and ascension; it is thus also the hour when Dante's purgation is completed and he ascends. Auden represents instead of this noblest hour the flawed and human time of dozing and daydreaming.) When Nones takes place in the sequence Horae Canonicae, it is followed by Vespers, a prose contrast of two types: Arcadians like the poet, who dream

of an Eden in the past, and Utopians, who work actively toward a secular
New Jerusalem in the future. Auden regards the first type as harmless,
the second as dangerous. The last two poems in the series become increasingly communal in feeling: Compline shows the body returning to
sleep, the mind asking to be spared: "That we, too, may come to the
picnic / With nothing to hide, join the dance" (CP, 485). Lauds is medieval
in tone and form, concerned no longer with individual guilt but with
communion: "Men of their neighbors become sensible; / God bless the
Realm, God bless the People: / In solitude, for company" (CP, 486). In later
poems the felt need for community becomes the basis of the central
myth of the City Without Walls and the mythologized House. In Whitsunday in Kirchstetten it is dramatized in the actual experience of the Mass and
of Pentecost interpreted as communion.

Auden never attempts to describe Heaven, though he says at the end
of In Praise of Limestone that he imagines it as a limestone landscape. He
certainly does not associate it with the stars, as Dante did; in fact, his
reaction to the stars is deflationary. In A Walk After Dark he finds the
"clockwork spectacle . . . Impressive in a slightly boring / Eighteenth-cen-
tury way" and decides that he is glad the "points in the sky" are middle-
aged, as he is: "It's cosier thinking of night / As more an Old People's
Home / Than a shed for a faultless machine, / That the red pre-Cambrian
light / Is gone like Imperial Rome / Or myself at seventeen" (CP, 267). In
The More Loving One he is even more antiromantic: "Looking up at the stars,
I know quite well / That for all they care, I can go to hell" (CP, 445); but if
equal affection cannot be, "Let the more loving one be me" (CP, 445). He
admires them, but does not really care; if they all disappeared "I should
learn to look at an empty sky / And feel its total dark sublime, /
Though this might take me a little time" (CP, 445). Auden rejects Milton's
God as firmly (though not as extensively) as does William Empson, and
dismisses with contempt in Whitsunday in Kirchstetten the notion of a "big
white Christian upstairs" who will bless our bombs; his speculations on
angels are usually tinged with amusement.[16] His imagination does not
often proceed beyond Dante's first point of contact with Heaven in the
Earthly Paradise, when the pilgrim reaches the supernatural condition of
innocence, his will is free, he needs neither Pope nor Emperor, and love
and law are one. But Auden develops the image of Eden with great sym-

bolic richness, and among its meanings a prefiguring of Heaven comes to be suggested.

In Auden's earlier work he takes a stern view of fantasy as either escapist or regressive, hence bad socially and psychologically. In *Paysage Moralisé* (1933) it is dreaming of islands that keeps us from rebuilding our cities. The dangers of fantasy and its consequences in neurosis are put most explicitly in *The Price* (1936): "Who can paint the vivid tree / And grass of phantasy? / But to create it and to guard / Shall be his whole reward" (CP, 129). By 1939 he regards fantasy more compassionately and describes its objects of yearning in terms that he will henceforth associate specifically with Eden: innocence, nudity, water, music, and dance. "Chilled by the Present, its gloom and its noise, / On waking we sigh for an ancient South, / A warm nude age of instinctive poise, / A taste of joy in an innocent mouth." We dream of a part "In the balls of the Future: each ritual maze / Has a musical plan, and a musical heart / Can faultlessly follow its faultless ways." But we, in our human condition, are "articled to error . . . / Were never nude and calm as a great door, / And never will be faultless like our fountains: / We live in freedom by necessity, / A mountain people dwelling among mountains" (CP, 156). A little later, in the last sonnet of *The Quest* sequence, the Garden is seen as the site of innocence, of choice, but chiefly of Grace: "All journeys die here: wish and weight are lifted," and the gaunt and great have blushed as they "felt their centre of volition shifted" (CP, 231). In *New Year Letter* the emphasis on choice is greater and the danger of being seduced by visions of Eden stressed. If an "accidental happiness" reveals to us the "field of Being" where we may be unconscious of Becoming and play with "Eternal Innocence," then we must beware of the temptation to remain there and avoid choice and change. For "perfect Being has ordained / It must be lost to be regained," and it is man's destiny to eat the fruit and depart. Hell, in fact, is the refusal to accept time, choose, and suffer (see CP, 177–78, discussed above, and CP, 195).

Caliban's speech in *The Sea and the Mirror* describes vividly two alternative types of regressive or escapist Edens, both leading to despair. In this period Auden taught a course at Swarthmore called "Romanticism from Rousseau to Hitler" and dealt severely with romantic Edens. Thus he writes in 1944 of Tennyson and Baudelaire: "Both felt themselves to be exiles from a lost paradise, . . . both shared the same nostalgia for the Happy Isles, *le vert paradis des amours enfantines*, to be reached only after long voyages over water; both imagine Eden in the same Rousseauistic terms; i.e., as a place of natural innocence rather than supernatural illumination" (*Forewords*, 231). As we have seen, the pursuit of false Edens is a major theme in *The Age of Anxiety*; as some of the characters perceive, hope lies only in renouncing fantasy and accepting our fallen selves in time.

The tone of *Age* is compassionate, however, and the Edenic fantasies at least produce a kind of communion, as well as characterizing each of the individuals. From this time on Auden tends to take a somewhat more tolerant view: though never forgetting their dangers, he suggests that dreams and longings for Eden are ineradicable, harmless if recognized for what they are and kept in their place, and fascinating as peculiarly human and unique in each individual. Much of *The Dyer's Hand* (1962) deals with this theme, in varying tones and applications. At the beginning he asserts that "so long as a man writes poetry or fiction, his dream of Eden is his own business, but the moment he starts writing literary criticism, honesty demands that he describe it to his readers, so that they may be in the position to judge his judgements" (*Dyer's Hand*, 6). He therefore gives his own answers to a questionnaire he once made up, which provides the relevant information in his case, from Landscape ("Limestone uplands like the Pennines plus a small region of igneous rocks with at least one extinct volcano. A precipitous and indented seacoast") to Language ("Of mixed origins like English, but highly inflected"), Religion ("Roman Catholic in an easygoing Mediterranean sort of way. Lots of local saints"), and Government ("Absolute monarchy, elected for life by lot"). Wish-games or Eden-dreams are dangerous if they are identified with a future New Jerusalem on earth (as by the Utopians of *Vespers*) or if they lead to a rejection of the self and consequent inability to desire. Nathanael West is the great expert on this latter state, Auden says, though it is also glimpsed in *Hamlet* and *Notes from Underground*. "As used by West, the cripple is, I believe, a symbolic projection of the state of wishful self-despair, the state of those who will not accept themselves in order to change themselves into what they would or should become, and justify their refusal by thinking that being what they are is uniquely horrible and uncurable" (*Dyer's Hand*, 243). In sharp contrast are the four English experts on Eden: Dickens, Oscar Wilde, Ronald Firbank, and P. G. Wodehouse. Auden discusses *Pickwick Papers* as example of the Eden-dream of a Christian shame-culture, going so far in pursuit of his argument as to denounce the Preamble to the American Constitution: "happiness is not a right; it is a duty. To the degree that we are unhappy, we are in sin. (And vice versa.) A duty cannot be pursued because its imperative applies to the present instant, not to some future date" (*Dyer's Hand*, 432).

All poems, Auden suggests in discussing Frost, may be described as collaborations between Ariel, inhabitant of a timeless, perfect, innocent Eden of pure play, and Prospero, who is concerned with the pain and disorder of temporal life and who tries, through revealing what life is really like, to free the reader from self-enchantment and deception. Ariel is concerned with beauty, Prospero with truth. Ariel has no passions, and nothing of serious importance can happen in his earthly paradise; Prospero, on the other hand, is constantly occupied with the questions, Who am I and Whom ought I to become? At the end of *The Dyer's Hand* Auden once more returns to this contrast (which is, of course, a development and specialization of his earlier versions in *The Sea and the Mirror*). Auden himself is clearly a Prospero-dominated poet, but Ariel never leaves him, however often he is set free, nor does Prospero ever get completely away from the Enchanted Island. The Island must be known for what it is and renounced in this life; but as dream of innocent prelapsarian Eden, or earthly paradise where love becomes law, realm of fantasy known as such, of play and reverent frivolity, it remains prominent in the poetry.

In the poetry the myth of Eden, together with the technique of psychic landscape, becomes a means of rehabilitating the genre of pastoral. *Ode to Gaea*, prefacing the series of *Bucolics*, celebrates the earthy point of view which sees "our good landscapes, . . . those woods where tigers chum with deer and no root dies," as simply "lies" (CP, 425). But the series itself seems to me highly successful as modern pastoral, rich in meanings and varied in tone. Perhaps the best of them all is *Streams*, which both enacts and expresses the Edenic themes we have been discussing. The poem begins by celebrating water above the other elements: "Air is boastful at times, earth slovenly, fire rude," but water is immaculate in bearing, playful, "pure being, perfect in music and movement." It makes communication possible, brings men together, "And *Homo Ludens*, surely, is your child, who make / fun of our feuds by opposing identical banks." Not even man can spoil it, for it "tells of a sort of world, quite other, / altogether different from this one / with its envies and passports, a polis like that / to which, in the name of scholars everywhere, / Gaston Paris pledged his allegiance / as Bismarck's siege-guns came within earshot" (CP, 434). The poem ends with a dream-vision recalling the allegorical procession Dante encountered in Eden, though this one is appropriately playful and mock-heroic: "the god of mortal doting" approaches in a cream and golden coach drawn by two baby locomotives, interrupting a croquet tournament; "With a wave of his torch he commanded a dance; / so round in a ring we flew, my dear on my right, / when I awoke" (CP, 435).

We are now at some remove from Dante in spirit. It may be said, I think, that Dante is supplemented (not supplanted) in his role of mentor in Auden's later career by—of all people—Paul Valéry. In view of Auden's oft-professed Francophobia, it was an unexpected and notably ecumenical gesture for him to choose a Frenchman for this role. Valéry's influence may often be detected in Auden's later definitions of poetry (as game, ritual, festival) and his awareness of its limitations. For Valéry, Auden says in an essay of 1969, Mallarmé was the example of the dedicated life, "a witness, a judge, a father, and a hallowed mentor." Auden continues: "I can vouch for at least one life in which Valéry does likewise. Whenever I am more than usually tormented by one of those horrid mental imps, *Contradiction, Obstination, Imitation, Lapsus, Brouillamini, Fange-d'Ame*, whenever I feel myself in danger of becoming un homme sérieux, it is on Valéry, un homme d'esprit if ever there was one, more often than on any other poet, I believe, that I call for aid" (Forewords, 366). "For Valéry, a poem ought to be a festival of the intellect, that is, a game, but a solemn, ordered, and significant game" (Forewords, 363). Valéry and Stravinsky, Auden remarks approvingly, "prefer the formal to the happy-go-lucky, an art which disintoxicates to an art which would bewitch, both have a horror of the pseudo-grandiloquent." He quotes Valéry frequently in The Dyer's Hand and The Viking Book of Aphorisms, and he was aware that Valéry's dawn meditations lay in the background of his own Prime and other poems.

To sum up, there is in Auden's poetry much less correlation to the Paradiso than to other parts of the Commedia. He rarely quotes it or alludes to it (except ironically, as in *The Love Feast*: "The Love that rules the sun and stars / Permits what He forbids," CP, 466). There is, however, a generalized resemblance in his images of communal joy as dancing in a circle. In *The Dyer's Hand* he remarks, "In a state of panic, a man runs round in circles by himself. In a state of joy, he links hands with others and they dance round in a circle together" (DH, 100). *Whitsunday in Kirchstetten* concludes, "if there when Grace dances, I should dance" (CP, 560). *Under Sirius* images Heaven briefly: "when in a carol under the appletrees / The reborn featly dance" (CP, 418). His most beautiful rendering of this image is perhaps that in *Compline*, notable for its basing of joy in rhythm and music from that of the heart to that of constellations and for its fusing of recognition of guilt with recognition of forgiveness. For once, he sees the whole cosmos as joyful dance, as his heart confesses "her part / In what happened to us from noon till three, / That constellations indeed / Sing of some hilarity beyond / All liking and happening" (CP, 484). He concludes with the prayer to "join the dance / As it moves in perichoresis, / Turns about the abiding tree" (CP, 485). Though he describes in prose his own experiences of the Vision of Eros and the Vision of Agape and professes belief in the supernatural as manifested in Grace, Providence, and the theological thrillers of Charles Williams, his poetic imagination seems to stop at the threshold with the Earthly Paradise.[17]

Auden's essay on Anger, in the symposium *The Seven Deadly Sins* (1962), provides a good example of his relation to Dante in this third and last period. There is no quotation from or reference to Dante; yet the whole discussion is pervaded by Dantean concepts and attitudes: specifically, those of the *Purgatorio*. Thus the essay begins in terms of the analysis we have seen Auden expound so often, based on *Purgatorio* 17: "Like all the sins except pride, anger is a perversion, caused by pride, of something in our nature which in itself is innocent, necessary to our existence and good." Natural anger, reaction to danger, is innocent; sinful anger "is one of our reactions to any threat, not to our existence, but to our fancy that our existence is more important than the existence of anybody or anything else." But Auden proceeds, not in theoretical terms but practical, considering various modern aspects of the sin. Thus "righteous anger" of the kind that underlies the doctrine of retributive punishment for criminals "is of the same discreditable kind which one can sometimes observe among parents and dog-owners, an anger at the lack of respect for his betters which the criminal has shown by daring to commit his crime. His real offence in the eyes of the authorities is not that he has done something wrong but that he has done something which THEY have forbidden." Finally, he expresses the wish that the clergy would explain "what the Church means by Hell and the Wrath of God." He notes first that the popular conception, by analogy with criminal law, makes God a cosmic policeman and is unchristian. The laws of spiritual life are not imposed, but are laws of our nature, like those of physics and physiology. "To speak of the Wrath of God cannot mean that God is Himself angry. It is the unpleasant experience of a creature, created to love and be happy, when he defies the laws of his spiritual nature. To believe in Hell as a possibility is to believe that God cannot or will not ever compel us to love and be happy. . . . If there are any souls in Hell, it is not because they have been sent there, but because Hell is where they insist upon being." That Dante lies behind this formulation is shown in Auden's earlier statement in his essay on Kierkegaard: "The Wrath of God is not a description of God in a certain state of feeling, but of the way in which I experience God if I distort or deny my relation to him. So Dante inscribed on the portals of Hell: 'Divine Power made me, Wisdom Supreme and Primal Love'—and Landor justly remarked about the Inferno that its inhabitants do not want to get out" (Forewords, 176).

To conclude: Auden throughout his career is primarily influenced by the Purgatorio, and especially by its analysis of Love as motive for both good and ill and of Envy as opposed to Charity and generosity. He interprets these doctrines in terms of modern psychology and biology, sometimes burlesquing them in the early verse but taking them very seriously indeed in his second stage. The Earthly Paradise becomes his chief image of joy in his third stage; except for images of dancing and music, it is as close as he will come to the Paradiso. Though at first he is preoccupied with false Edens as images of regression and irresponsibility, he comes to regard Eden-fantasies more indulgently as part of the precious individuality of each unique human being and play in general as part of the distinctive humanity of homo ludens. Hell Auden regards as a logical possibility, but he does not dwell on it, and images from the Inferno are rare in his work. The Devil in the earlier verse is usually God in disguise (repressed instincts) or the archetypal Blakean rebel who "has broken parole and arisen" to destroy conventional society, or the Goethean spirit of doubt and denial who leads us to reject the world of Time in which we must exist: "The shadow just behind the shoulder / Claiming it's wicked to grow older." In spite of himself, "He has to make the here and now / As marvellous as he knows how." But he has "no positive existence"; he is only "a recurrent state / Of fear and faithlessness and hate," and his function is "to push us into grace" (CP, 168–69).

In spite of this emphasis on the *Purgatorio*, the tone of Auden's work is rarely penitential. Instead, it moves from the gaiety and exuberance of the best early pieces to the joy and "reverent frivolity" of the later ones. There is an interesting contrast here with Eliot, whose tone is penitential in most of his greatest poetry, but whose imagination dwells most deeply on the supernatural realms of the *Inferno* and *Paradiso*. Auden's imagination remains attached to the earth's surface, going neither underground nor into the heavens, and his preoccupations are human, moral, and dramatic. His theme may be said to be the definition of man as the only creature that exists fully in Time or, alternatively, of Time as the essential human condition. Auden rarely attempts terza rima, nor are there many specifically Dantesque images or structures in his work.[18] But Dante is always present as chief mentor, model, and judge, with a changing group of assistants ranging from the great rebels Blake and Rimbaud to Valéry, the dedicated aesthete who went beyond poetry. As pilgrim, Auden had no Virgil and no Beatrice (Kierkegaard and Charles Williams being perhaps the nearest equivalents), and his spiritual journey corresponds only to the central one of Dante's three. But his work is not unworthy of the comparison.

NOTES

1. *The Latin Works of Dante Alighieri* (London: J. M. Dent, 1904), p. 350.

2. W. H. Auden, *The Dyer's Hand* (New York: Random House, 1962), pp. 198, 206, 145; see also pp. 176–77.

3. W. H. Auden, *Collected Poems* (New York: Random House, 1976), p. 300. Hereafter called CP.

4. W. H. Auden, *The English Auden*, ed. Edward Mendelson (New York: Random House, 1977), p. 62. Hereafter called TEA.

5. It was published for the first time, with an excellent commentary, by Lucy S. McDiarmid: "W. H. Auden's 'In the Year of my Youth,'" R. E. S. 29 (1978): 267–312.

For further discussion, see Edward Mendelson, *Early Auden* (New York: Viking, 1981), pp. 133–34, 148–51.

6. Separately published in *The Criterion*, October 1931.

7. W. H. Auden and Christopher Isherwood, *The Dog Beneath the Skin, or, Where is Francis?* (New York: Random House, 1935). Hereafter called *Dog*.

8. "Crisis," *Atlantic* CLXIV, 3 (September, 1939): 358–59.

9. *Purgatorio* 14.85–87. Auden always uses the Temple Classics editions of Dante, which have the Italian and an English translation on facing pages. The *Purgatorio* translation here quoted is by Thomas Okey (London: J. M. Dent & Sons, 1901). Though Auden's Italian was fluent, he usually quotes the English translation.

10. That Auden seriously and repeatedly suggests an analogy between the damned and the neurotic is made most explicit in a late essay on the sin of Anger. Hell, he says, is a possibility if we believe that God cannot or will not ever compel us to love and be happy: "The analogy which occurs to me is with neurosis . . . a neurotic, an alcoholic, let us say, is not happy; on the contrary, he suffers terribly, yet no one can relieve his suffering without his consent and this he so often withholds. He insists on suffering because his ego cannot bear the pain of facing reality and the diminution of self-importance which a cure would involve. If there are any souls in Hell, it is not because they have been sent there, but because Hell is where they insist upon being." W. H. Auden, "Anger," in *The Seven Deadly Sins*, edited by Raymond Mortimer (New York: William Morrow and Co., 1962), p. 87.

11. D. A. Stauffer, ed., *The Intent of the Critic* (Princeton: Princeton University Press, 1941), p. 132.

12. Cited in W. H. Auden, *The Double Man* (New York: Random House, 1941), pp. 141, 158–59. Auden cites both passages also in *The Dyer's Hand*, pp. 130, 230.

13. Auden, *Double Man*, p. 76. Auden cites E. M. Forster in *I Believe* as source for da Todi, but he must have been familiar long before with the quotation in Italian, because it is set as an epigraph to the Temple Classics *Purgatorio*. As early as 1947 he recommends D'Arcy's *Mind and Heart of Love*, a Catholic study that joins Eros and Agape in the concept of *Caritas* (*New York Times*, 29 June 1947). In 1950 he writes that there "has been a tendency to see the notion of love as eros or desire for getting and the notion of love as agape or free-giving as incompatible opposites and to identify them with Paganism and Christianity respectively. Such a view seems to me a revival of the Manichean heresy which denies the goodness of the natural order." Quoted by John Fuller, *A Reader's Guide to W. H. Auden* (New York: Farrar, Straus & Giroux, 1970), p. 232.

14. Jerome Mazzaro, *Profile of Robert Lowell* (Columbus, Ohio: Charles E. Merrill Co., 1971), p. 68.

15. W. H. Auden, *Forewords and Afterwords* (New York: Random House, 1973), p. 192. Hereafter called *Forewords*.

16. Auden, *Forewords*, p. 255; *A Certain World* (New York: Random House, 1970), p. 22.

17. See Auden's essay, "The Protestant Mystics," in *Forewords*, especially pp. 68–70. Reviewing *The Portable Dante* in 1947, Auden remarks that Eliot's lines in *Little Gidding* are the best imitation of Dante in English and concludes amusingly by advising the reader that "just in case he is going to be saved, he should start learning Italian, because English may be the language of Heaven, but in the Earthly Paradise, I am quite sure, nothing but Italian will be spoken or sung."

18. In terza rima are Antonio's speech in *The Sea and the Mirror*, *Family Ghosts*, *Diaspora*; in variations of it are *Alone* and *One Circumlocution*. There is a vaguely Dantesque dimension to two of the opera libretti: in *The Rake's Progress* Tom is saved from Nick Shadow by Anne, a kind of Beatrice-figure, and in *Elegy for Young Lovers* false Edens are identified with Hell.

GLAUCO CAMBON

Wallace Stevens's Dialogue with Dante

*When the superstructures crumble, the common foundation
of human sentience and imagination is exposed beneath.*
George Santayana, *The Sense of Beauty*

I like to think of Wallace Stevens walking from bar to bar in his native
Reading, Pennsylvania, one evening of October 1900, to ask the bartend-
ers about neighborhood fellows like "Mike Angelo, Butch Petrarch,
Sammy Dante."[1] Just as happens in so many of his poems, his letters and
the excerpts of an early journal reveal the imp in him hand in hand with
the meditative thinker, whose joy it is intently to play with the inexhaust-
ible object of thought so that it may never cease to surprise the mind's
eye. In a less impish form, *gai saber* flavors another one of his sporadic
references to Dante Alighieri in the *Letters*: "Yesterday I bought a little
volume called the 'Notebooks' of Matthew Arnold. It is made up of quotations jotted down by him from day to day, and of lists of various books
to be read at various times. The quotations are in a half-dozen different
languages. (It gives me a sort of learned delight to guess at the Latin ones;
and last night I hunted all through Dante for translations of several Italian
ones)" (p. 101). No doubt this happy game would yield him, decades
later, the source for a truncated Dantean quote in stanza 10 of *Examination
of a Hero in Time of War*:

102

And if the phenomenon, magnified, is
Further magnified, *sua voluntate*,
Beyond his circumstance . . .[2]

The famous line from *Paradiso* 3.85, so exemplary to Arnold for its "high seriousness," is mischievously broken up and juggled around to mean the contrary of what it said in its Italian context, for Stevens replaces God's will with man's will.

The mischievousness stood Stevens in good stead. How else was he going to cope with the sometimes stifling solemnity with which much scholarship has managed to envelop Dante and his work? The liberty of the artist, and especially of such a learned artist as Wallace Stevens was, combines playfulness and profundity, that is to say a measure of irreverence toward the very models he looks up to—Dante being an early one for Wallace Stevens, as we may already gather from a journal entry of 23 May 1899: "Those who say that poetry is now the peculiar province of women say so because their ideas about poetry are effeminate. Homer, Dante, Shakespeare, Milton, Keats, Browning, much of Tennyson—these are your man-poets. Silly verse is always the work of silly men. Poetry itself is unchanged" (*Letters*, 26). Overlooking the quantum of irrelevant male chauvinism that this diary entry betrays (and Stevens would have been the first to admit that Sappho, Vittoria Colonna, or Emily Dickinson were not silly poets), we shall find the relevant import, regarding Dante's significance, beautifully confirmed and expanded half a century later, in the first of the essays that make up *The Necessary Angel*.[3] Here is the excerpt in point:

Suppose we try, now, to construct the figure of a poet, a possible poet. He cannot be a charioteer traversing vacant space, however ethereal. He must have lived all of the last two thousand years, and longer, and he must have instructed himself, as best he could, as he went along. He will have thought that Virgil, Dante, Shakespeare, Milton placed themselves in remote lands and in remote ages; that their men and women were dead—and not the dead lying in the earth, but the dead still living in their remote lands and in their remote ages, and living in the earth or under it, or in the heavens—and he will wonder at those huge imaginations, in which what is remote becomes near, and what is dead lives with an intensity beyond any experience in life.

Historical placement by no means dims the aesthetic exemplariness of Dante (and of the other members of the exclusive company who embody verbal imagination at its best) for the ideal poet of the new age Stevens is describing here; and the use this hypothetical new poet is supposed to make of those formidable examples is conceived in a way that calls to mind Whitman on the one hand, Eliot on the other. He knows his ancestors but he asserts his freedom, in a dialectical continuity which excludes both the blanket rejections of extremist futurism and the cramping submission of academic classicism. Above all, the modern poet shall eschew the pitfall of heroic solemnity, for "he knows perfectly that he cannot be too noble a rider, that he cannot rise up loftily in helmet and armor on a horse of imposing bronze. He will think again of Milton and of what was said about him" (NR, 24). One knows one's fathers in order to match the strength of their accomplishment, not certainly to parrot their posture or repeat what they already unimprovably did in the timeliness of their historical circumstances. If so conceived, historical perspective will be liberating rather than an enslaving factor for the new artist, and whatever Stevens has to say here of the dreamed-of new poet applies to him just as well.

Utterly un-Dantesque as the author of *Thirteen Ways of Looking at a Blackbird* sounds, he still did have Dante as one of his inner interlocutors, whether in the reflective process of defining poetry or in the direct practice of the art; and I for one find it hard to separate the two activities in Stevens's case, where actual poetry and discursive poetics tend constantly to merge. The sporadic tessellation of quotes from Dante is by no means the basic clue to the complex bond between the modern American "dandy" of poetry (as he was sometimes called) and the stern medieval Florentine who was in a few respects his exact opposite. Such tessellation, in fact, occurs seldom if ever in Stevens, much more seldom than in poets like his contemporaries Yeats, Eliot, Pound, or Montale, who in their different ways are all closer to Dante's own ideology, and for that reason feel freer to ransack Dante's opus (since they all do to that opus what the medieval Christians did to Roman temples to build their basilicas). I might even delude myself by thinking that a line like

Freedom is like a man who kills himself

in *Dutch Graves in Bucks County* intentionally echoes Virgil's words to Cato the noble suicide in *Purgatorio* 1:

Libertà va cercando, ch'è sì cara
come sa chi per lei vita rifiuta

(Freedom is what he seeks, the dearest boon
as those well know who for its sake reject life itself.)[4]

I let it stand at any rate as a matter of high probability, given the wide currency of the *Divine Comedy* passage involved.

But, I beg to insist, if the parameter of Dante's relevance to Stevens's poetics were to be given just by the frequency of Stevens's Dantean quotations, it would make Dante extremely marginal to the American poet's work—an inference which Stevens's own statements in *The Necessary Angel* compel us to discard. Nor would it pay to look for direct reverberations of Dante's spare style in the sumptuous rhetoric that drapes so much of Stevens's poetic meditation. That rhetoric stems from Elizabethan, Miltonic, Wordsworthian, and even Shelleyan patterns, while the contrapuntal whimsicality in which Stevens also delights has its antecedents in the Elizabethan ditty, in Lewis Carroll's nonsense verse, and in Jules Laforgue's Pierrotesque wit, as well as in American colloquial mannerisms. Here again the Dantesque affinities of Yeats, Eliot, and Pound stand out by sheer contrast with Stevens's different stylistic orientation, which points to Elizabethan, Romantic, and French *symboliste* magnets. Besides, Stevens's swaying between the vatic and the playful voice, so typical of him as to be a signature, could never come off without the sustaining undertone of American speech, a component of primary importance. The triumph of that acrobatic modulation is to be heard in *The Man with a Blue Guitar*.

It is the use of thematic cues that defines Stevens's responsiveness to Dante in matters of poetic practice. When, for instance, we come across the following initial stanzas, from *The Hand as a Being*:

In the first canto of the final canticle,
Too conscious of too many things at once,
Our man beheld the naked, nameless dame,

Seized her and wondered: why beneath the tree
She held her hand before him in the air,
For him to see, wove round her glittering hair,　　　　　　　[CP, 271]

we cannot help realizing that Stevens is appropriating a specific episode from the *Divine Comedy* for his own desecrating purposes. The "first canto of the final canticle" of course refers to *Paradiso* 1, where the pilgrim of the Beyond, by now alone with Beatrice, experiences the shared liftoff into heaven that she makes possible, and in the process is thoroughly confused by the overpowering novelty and radiance of a sun-flooded sky astir with cosmic music. Lest we miss the reference, Stevens reiterates his cue two more times, by repeating the line "In the first canto" in the third and again in the sixth of the seven tercets that make up this strange poem. Likewise, the line depicting our pilgrim's bewilderment at the sudden exposure to the unwonted paradisal situation ("Too conscious . . .") recurs with the other one in Tercet 3. The very verse, for a change, dances to Dante's tune: it is musically terse and spare, vatically sustained, and arranged in tercets that do not lack occasional rhyme—a concomitant reminder of the poem's literary origin.

But Stevens is conjuring Dante in order to exorcise him, or at least that aspect of his myth which Stevens heartily rejects—the notion that Paradise should be "up there," and bodiless, mystical, desexualized. Stevens has no use for a merely intellectualized eros, or for a bliss that is not "accessible bliss." Consequently, not only does he turn the tables against hyperspiritualized Beatrice by making her "naked" and "nameless," but he is also juggling his Dantean reference in another respect, by telescoping the situation described in *Paradiso* 1 with the situation obtaining toward the end of *Purgatorio*, where Dante has himself confront an imperious Beatrice in the green scenery of a reattained Eden on top of the purifying mountain island. In Dante's version of Paradise regained, the tree stands for what every reader of the Bible knows, and it plays a conspicuous part in the allegorical charade of sacred and profane history that is enacted for the pilgrim's benefit. In Stevens's mischievous rewriting of the episode, the tree is divested of its formidable implications:

Her hand composed him and composed the tree.

The wind had seized the tree and ha, and ha,
It held the shivering, the shaken limbs,
Then bathed its body in the leaping lake.

This lady is imperious, too, in her way, and she has magical powers of sorts; she "composes" the tree to suit her antitranscendent purposes, she reconciles man and tree with her hand on which everything finally focuses, and the ritual action unleashes the hilarity of an elvish wind which bloweth here of all places, providentially to shake any inhibitive function off the branches of the tree of knowledge and make it possible for the two characters—a new Adam and a perennial Eve—to sleep together under its benevolent shade. The only knowledge this once forbidding tree now imparts will be serene, fruitful, carnal yet deeply human, not brutish:

To the ruddier bushes at the garden's end.
Of her, of her alone at last he knew
And lay beside her underneath the tree.

He, Everyman, had been "conscious of too many things," had allowed extraneous superstructures of thought, nasty taboos and theological figments, to distract him from the one thing that mattered, the love and enjoyment of Eve-Everywoman, of Alma Tellus, of what this world has to offer. This is the innocence, and the science, that counts. The theme already rang out in *Sunday Morning*, and it will ring out again in *Auroras of Autumn*.

An intimacy with the earth ("confidence in the world," as one essay in *Opus Posthumous* has it), a reconsecration of the flesh, a rerooting of the mind in its natural ambience (for which see also *The Comedian as the Letter C*), point to an authentic ecology of mind. The lady's hand, even in the title, becomes a synecdoche of poetry's healing power. The poem under examination, then, has even this in common with its Dantean source to which it sets up a precise antitype: that it allegorizes a narrative incident without violating the intense life of the letter. Rather than allegories, these are, in Auerbach's words, *figurae* of human destiny. We see, in conclusion, that Stevens's irreverence is part of a new reverence, that he desecrates to reconsecrate. Dante the poetical character and Beatrice find their fulfillment in flying from the earth into the heavenly spheres, at the call of an inverted gravity; Stevens's figural personae resist that push and redirect it to earth. But for all that, Stevens is not quite parodying Dante. He is emulating him on his own ground because Dante is among the few masters of his craft that count, and between Stevens and the atrabilious Florentine there should be (as Pound put it with regard to Whitman) "a pact."

We remember that, in *The Imagination as Value*, the American poet who liked Dante's poetry better than his eschatology said: "the great poems of heaven and hell have been written and the great poem of the earth remains to be written" (NR, 142). If Dante and Milton had written the conclusive epics of the transcendent, Wallace Stevens looked forward to the poet of the immanence epos, to the humanist poem, and spent a lifetime himself writing what could be termed its first formulation, or, to extrapolate from his own language, the "notes toward a supreme fiction." For what is *Notes* if not the preliminary sketch of the great poem of the earth, under the form of an *ars poetica*? And does not the theme persist through resourceful modulations from *Sunday Morning* to *The Comedian as the Letter C*, *Esthétique du Mal*, and *Credences of Summer*? "The greatest poverty is not to live / In a physical world," says the beginning of *Esthétique*'s conclusion, and the "fat girl, terrestrial, my summer, my night" in the last poem of *Notes Toward a Supreme Fiction* figures forth, according to Stevens himself, earth anthropomorphized as woman.[5] Yet, just as happens in *The Hand as a Being*, this vindication of terrestrial and carnal reality against the sublimations of a transcendent theology takes place in forms directly reminiscent of the one "great poem of heaven and hell" that had radically voiced those sublimations.

As I pointed out thirty years ago, on the strength of the poetical text alone, *Notes Toward a Supreme Fiction* is a movement, articulated in three parts, toward the paradisal fulfillment of love and knowledge on earth, the only possible paradise.[6] Infernal overtones are not lacking in Part 1 (*It Must Be Abstract*) where human alienation from the purity of Nature's "first idea" is intermittently deplored, while purgatorial echoes seem to crop up in Part 2 (*It Must Change*) where the approach of metaphor to reality is developed, and clear paradisal notes ring out in Part 3 (*It Must Give Pleasure*) where we hear of the reconciliation of rational and irrational, of nature and "first idea" (equals existence and essence), of knowledge and joy, of human and angelic powers, of flesh and spirit, earth and sky. Under the guise of an *ars poetica*, Stevens has given us his poetical metaphysics and epistemology, and his system of values. The trajectory unfolds from the death of the gods (stripping reality bare of its mythological superstructures) to the rebirth of reality in a liberated consciousness.

As in the *Divine Comedy*, the triadic structure of the thematic macrocosm mirrors itself in the microcosm of verse, since all the poems that make up the sequence are couched in tercets, albeit unrhymed, and Dante's preoccupation with structural numerology is also reflected in the fact that each of the three parts consists of ten poems. The impressionist brushwork fleshes out a didactic and occasionally vatic stance, for Stevens considers poetry a cognitive activity, and philosophy—though not Thomistic or Aristotelian—is obviously involved in the process. Figural episodes of a sort punctuate the rhapsody: Ozymandias and Nanzia Nunzio, the virgin Bawda, the planter, the Canon Aspirin. Stevens had to use Dante's weapons to turn Dante's world upside down. It could be argued that the triadic pattern stems from Hegel no less than Dante, for Stevens himself talks of a dialectical movement in the poetry of perception, and what's more, he frequently uses that paradigm in his verse. But it does not invalidate my point about Stevens's Dantesque propensities; they may well blend with others in the alchemy of the word, and certainly in *Notes* the referential pattern is prominently Dantean. In *Credences of Summer* he likewise resorts to a deftly transposed Dantean cue to illustrate poetically the (triadic) phenomenology of perception:

> Three times the concentred self takes hold, three times
> The thrice concentred self, having possessed
> The object, grips it in savage scrutiny.   [CP, 376]

It does not take long to identify the cue in *Purgatorio*:

> Oi ombre vane, fuor che ne l'aspetto!
> tre volte dietro lei le braccia avvinsi,
> e tante mi tornai con esse al petto.   [2.79–81]

> (Oh empty shades, except in appearance!
> Three times I reached out to clasp this one,
> and as many I folded my arms back on my chest.)

Dante the pilgrim is trying to embrace the soul of his old friend Casella, and Dante the poet chooses to heighten the sense of frustration as well as the dignity accruing to the incident by telling it in the very terms in which his master and guide Virgil had once told the story of Aeneas vainly trying to embrace the ghost of his wife Creusa in *Aeneid*:

> ter conatus ibi collo dare bracchia circum,
> ter frustra comprensa manus effugit imago,
> par levibus ventis volucrique simillima somno.   [2.79–94]

> (Three times there I tried to throw my arms around her neck,
> three times the image eluded my clutching hands,
> like a light wind and most like a fleeting dream.)

Virgil in turn, for similar purposes, took the rhetorical topos from *Odyssey* 11, where Odysseus tries to embrace the phantom of his mother; and we must consider the Stevensian use of that topos no mere Dantesque reference, but a compound one involving the whole tradition that reiterates the tale of pathetic frustration. Since Stevens is refuting the ontology of shadows and insists on the tangible as an object of poetry and belief, on the "rock of summer," his deft reworking of the Homeric-Virgilian-Dantesque topos acquires the same meaning that the paradisal allusion has in *The Hand as a Being*: it contributes to the desired emphasis on an immanent approach. Reality is graspable, unlike the ghosts which the old Christian dispensation foisted on our credulity.

No wonder that we should find the same polemic against ascetic and transcendent Christianity in *Esthétique du Mal*, where the aesthetic meaning of pain and evil is explored partly by outright statement and counter-statement, partly through capsule lives of the relevant poets, like Leopardi,[7] Dante, and possibly Rimbaud and Baudelaire (Góngora is briefly brought into the picture as "the Spaniard of the rose"). Dante appears unequivocally in Part 3 to supply the occasion for an antiChristian tirade, and as if to pinpoint the reference, the verse clusters into tercets (the only part of the poem where this happens):

> His firm stanzas hang like hives in hell
> Or what hell was, since now both heaven and hell
> Are one, and here, O terra infidel.

Dante as poet is exempted from the fairly Nietzschean condemnation of Christian values, the "too, too human god, self-pity's kin," who can only "weaken our fate" and "relieve us of woe both great / And small," thus imposing on us a spiritually "uncourageous genesis." Stoic fortitude and acceptance of the human condition are contrasted to the allegedly corrupting sentimentalities of Christianity, which in turn account for the rise of hell's sick superstition and of the correlative alienated conception of paradise that is really a fool's paradise. By the light of Stoic humanism, instead,

> the health of the world might be enough,

and

> It seems as if the honey of common summer
> Might be enough, as if the golden combs
> Were part of a sustenance itself enough,

for

> hell, so modified, had disappeared

and

> pain, no longer satanic mimicry,
> could be borne,

in which case

> we were sure to find our way

much like the Dantean pilgrim persona at the outset of *Inferno* under Virgil's guidance; but for opposite reasons, because our version of the Dark Wood is precisely the alienated theology and ethics to which Dante looked for salvation and from which we have been emerging under the humanist dispensation.

Dante's poetry elicits admiration for its formal tautness ("firm stanzas") and imaginative delight ("hives"), yet is iconically projected into an incongruous ambience, for beehives should be hanging somewhere else than in hell's gothic dungeons, and this is what is blamed on Christian theology ("The fault lies with an over-human god," Christ being in the ecclesiastical conception what Nietzsche would have called "menschlich, allzumenschlich," a debilitating idea which mortifies the intellect and inhibits the senses and the body).

Since, as Stevens's *Adagia* have it,[8] "poetry is a health," we may safely assume that the honey distilled by Dante's craft was itself an antidote, or the beginning of a liberation, and in any case poetry as such is not timebound even if the underlying ideology is—a conception Stevens shares with Croce and, more importantly, with Santayana.[9] The poem's imagery bears it out, for the "hives" of line 1 reappear with a vengeance in the sixth of these seven tercets as "honey of common summer" and "golden combs ... part of a sustenance itself enough," at which point Dante's poetry is equated with great poetry in general and with the imagination as a life-affirming force. We remember that *The Necessary Angel*, while disclaiming any political function for the poet, says that he helps us to live, that this indeed is poetry's existential use. We also remember, from the same book, an eloquent passage in *The Figure of the Youth as Virile Poet*: "The indirect purpose or, perhaps, it would be better to say, inverted effect of soliloquies in hell and of most celestial poems ... seems to be to produce an agreement with reality" (NR, 57). Which is another way of saying that it may be worthwhile for the modern secularized spirit to crawl into the *Inferno*'s repulsive vaults in order to snatch the honey Dante gathered there. To accomplish this, we need no transcendental guide like Virgil, certainly not if his task be to detail an ideological salvation plan for us bewildered wards; the poet, according to Stevens, can save us not by leading "people out of the confusion in which they find themselves," but simply by sharing his imagination with us, the people, and in so doing he will provide a viable alternative world. Poetry is "a violence within" that counteracts a violence without, a saving counterpressure; it need not prescribe a course of action. "Dante himself," Stevens says in *The Noble Rider and the Sound of Words*, "in Purgatory and Paradise was still the voice of the Middle Ages but not through fulfilling any social obligation" (NR, 28–29).

Stevens resolutely refuses any notion of political engagement as a standard or prerequisite for poetry, yet is far from relegating the function of poetry to a passive individual epicureanism, for he sees it as a liberating force, indeed as a form of knowledge to be shared. "No politician can command the imagination," (NR, 28) because, as *Notes Toward a Supreme Fiction* has it, "to impose is not to discover," and "to know the summer" calls for a total openness and purity of the mind, which must shed its preconceived notions in the encounter with reality. That is exactly what enabled Stevens himself to accept Dante's accomplishment while rejecting the Christian metaphysical bias which provided Dante with a great deal of his building materials. This humanist appraisal of Dante's work recalls Blake's, Blake being an apposite reference if we listen to Tercet 1 of *Esthétique du Mal* ("now both heaven and hell / Are one, and here"). Stevens likewise knows "that men in general do not create in light and warmth alone. They create in darkness and coldness. They create when they are hopeless, in the midst of antagonisms, when they are wrong, when their powers are no longer subject to their control."[10] Which makes a substantial part of the theme of *Esthétique du Mal* and of Stevens's reasons for liking such a temperamentally, historically, and ideologically different writer as Dante was.

Stevens's humanism cannot be accused of the simplistic reductions from which the contemporary predicament has weaned even the most stubborn optimists among us. He knows of the subtle providential dialectic that can operate in creative lives, as *Esthétique* shows. And just as he refutes the idea of an anthropomorphic God, he practices an anthropological exorcism against the metaphysical myth of evil:

> The genius of misfortune
> Is not a sentimentalist. He is
> That evil, that evil in the self, from which
> In desperate hallow, rugged gesture, fault
> Falls out on everything: the genius of
> The mind, which is our being, wrong and wrong,
> The genius of the body, which is our world,
> Spent in the false engagements of the mind.[11]

In other words, hell is not denied, but "modified," channeled into the dialectics of life, just as Mephistopheles, "*der Geist der stets verneint*," was a vital part of Faust's redemptive ordeal. Stevens acknowledges the presence of evil and pain in the world ("We are not / At the center of a diamond"). He rebuts any facile optimism that would explain them away, and he thinks that the evil in us—a man-centered reality—must be faced without recourse to supernatural fictions. The flowers of evil are of our own making, a product of our own alienation.

Satan's death, says Esthétique, Part 8, "was a tragedy / For the imagination," considering what the Satanic myth had done for poets like Dante, Milton, or Goethe. The death of Satan was unspectacular; "he was denied." The advent of rationalism kills the myth of personified evil, and along with it many celestial myths ("blue phenomena"), for to kill Satan is also to kill God, transcendence for transcendence, nether and upper. Once the "poor phantoms" of mythic imagination are dispelled by reason, once Vico's "age of the gods" and "age of heroes" wane into the "age of men," man confronts a bare scene and he feels imaginatively deprived, since to imagine is to personify. Yet this is just a new beginning, for

> the tragedy . . . may have begun,
> Again, in the imagination's new beginning,
> In the yes of the realist spoken because he must
> Say yes, spoken because under every no
> Lay a passion for yes that had never been broken.

Stevens plays on the word "tragedy" to make it mean "disaster" the first time and "drama of poetry" the second time it appears in the part of Esthétique we have been quoting. In your end is my beginning, says the emancipated mind to the fabulous creatures of its own archaic making; the imagination is not irretrievably bound to its own anthropomorphic phase, for the anthropomorphic hypostases of primitive or fanatical faith, angels and demons, God and Satan alike, vanish only to make way for the experience of a reality that, stripped of such superstructures, will dawn as a new planet on the mind. The new "supreme fiction" will then take place, although or rather because the old mythologies are dead. Meanwhile there is, of course, the interval of horrid emptiness:

> To see the gods dispelled in mid-air and dissolve like clouds is one of the great human experiences. . . . It is simply that they came to nothing. Since we have always shared all things with them and have always had a part of their strength and, certainly, all of their knowledge, we shared likewise this experience of annihilation. It was their annihilation, not ours, and yet it left us feeling that in a mea-

sure, we, too, had been annihilated. It left us feeling dispossessed and alone, in a solitude, like children without parents, in a home that seemed deserted. . . . [OP, 206–7]

This is the experience that Dante did not have, and that men like Leopardi, Arnold, and Stevens were historically suited to express. Toward the end of his life Stevens expressed it most starkly, in *Auroras of Autumn II*:

> Farewell to an idea . . . A cabin stands,
> Deserted, on a beach. It is white . . .
> A darkness gathers though it does not fall
>
> And the whiteness grows less vivid on the wall.
> The man who is walking turns blankly on the sand.
> He observes how the north is always enlarging the change,
>
> With its frigid brilliances, its blue-red sweeps
> And gusts of great enkindlings, its polar green,
> The color of ice and fire and solitude.   [CP, 412]

Auroras may very well be one of Stevens's highest accomplishments and here too he takes his bearings from the great tradition of which Dante is a prominent part and which supplies him with his prosodic tools, the "firm stanzas" that "hang like hives" not in hell, but in the weird emptiness created by the mind's ruthless palimpsest.

As the series begins it is as if consciousness had come to a zero point, a nothingness of its own making. Its objective correlative is the winter sky of New England, where the Northern Lights enact phantasmagorias that evoke those of the mind itself (much as the timeless shape of constellations had suggested figures and names of many a myth to remote generations of stargazing cartographers). In the eerie beauty of that phantom pageantry the human imagination projects its own fables, and instant theogony is followed by instant *Goetterdaemmerung*. The serpent of Poem No. I (akin to Paul Valéry's *Ebauche d'un serpent*[12]), while it is visually suggested by the sinuous drapings of the northern lights, actually calls to mind the insidious power of doubt and denial, that which in the long run destroyed faith in the biblical fable of genesis or in any other. The father of Poem No. IV is the anthropomorphic God of so many mythologies, while the mother of the following poem is the essence of every matriarchal deity, and the two principles combine in Poem V to invite mankind to a phantom feast.

Poem No. I of *Notes Toward a Supreme Fiction* had warned the intent "ephebe" against postulating for any cosmogony or cosmology "a voluminous master folded in his fire," and here in *Auroras* the key word *master* recurs as a countersign to father, which has an obvious theological import (to be occasionally glimpsed without its anthropomorphic burden in kindred expressions from other Stevensian works, like *The Red Fern*: there we find a "furiously burning father-fire"). Since the father of Poem No. IV "sits / In space, wherever he sits" (lines 2–3), then "Now . . . sits in quiet and green-a-day" and "assumes the great speeds of space" (lines 10–11), to be finally addressed by the persona in lines 19–20 as "Master O Master seated by the fire / And yet in space," he denotes God as creative principle, modeled on the procreative and dominant power of the earthly fathers, a clear patriarchal myth. His dominance continues, as manifested through art and with the help of the feminine godhead (Mary-Venus-Cybele-Ishtar) in Poem V, but in Poem VII he is openly decreated (to use Stevens's own term as borrowed from Simone Weil);[13] in other words, he is unmasked for the anthropomorphic figment he is and reduced to his source in the human mind, namely the imagination, the true "father-fire."

That demystifying process is conveyed by the exact semantic, lexical, and iconic echoes which link Poem VII to Poem IV. If in Poem IV it is the father and master that "sits" in what at the end turns out to be a throne appropriate to kings and gods, in Poem VII it is the "imagination" that "sits enthroned" (line 1), "as grim as it is benevolent" (line 2). In Poem IV the divine father figure "leaps from heaven to heaven more rapidly / Than bad angels leap from heaven to hell in flames" (lines 8–9); in Poem VII the imagination is called a "goat-leaper, crystalled and luminous, sitting / In highest night" (lines 6–7), and further on it "leaps through us, through all our heavens leaps, / Extinguishing our planets, . . . one by one" (lines 13–14). In the same way, the mother principle becomes one and the same thing with the gentler, earthbound, "innocent" aspect of sensibility in Poem VIII (lines 22–24). The decreation, the unmasking, the anthropological reduction of key anthropomorphic projections to their source in the mind's fabulating activity, validates those fables aesthetically in retrospect.

Because, as the beginning of Poem IV has it, "the cancelings, The negations are never final," the death of the gods as we saw need not be the death of the imagination itself, which created them all in man's image; men live by the imagination and not by bread alone. Stevens is showing again how poetry can arise from the very destruction of that which fed poetry for ages, namely, mythology—a Leopardian theme he develops in his own register.[14] When finally the mind sees through itself, tearing apart the luminous veil of its own fables (light engendering darkness, extinguishing planets, as in Poem VII), reality dawns, refreshed, to fill the awesome emptiness. That, as I said, is a Leopardian, not a Dantean theme; but it unfolds against Dante's countertheme of the ascent into heaven and of the contemplation of God the Unmoved Mover of the universe:

> Master O master seated by the fire
> And yet in space and *motionless* and yet
> Of *motion* the ever-brightening *origin*   [CP, 414]

Correlatively, the feminine godhead principle that adorns the last cantos of Dante's *Paradiso* as Mary the Virgin Mother also graces Poem V of *Auroras*—where a twilight of the gods is rehearsed to offset Dante's dazzling theophanies.

If Stevens's is a poetry of disenchantment and immanence while Dante's was a poetry of miracle-fed faith, both authors set store by what the modern American calls the "supreme poetry," the "poetry of thought"[15]—not the same thing as philosophy versified. It is, rather, the drama of thought made palpable in its unfolding; and in both cases the movement is through and away from the delusions of fiction mistaken for reality, toward a truth that satisfies because it cannot be exhausted—a truth that exceeds even the "high imagination" (*Paradiso* 33.142) striving to grasp it and that accordingly keeps challenging the mind to mirror it in a "supreme fiction." Since both poets rely on a realist ontology of sorts, regardless of the wide gap between the medieval conception of a finalist, animated, theocentric universe and the dismantled hulk modern science has left us for a cosmos, here Dante and Stevens converge from their opposite sides of the divide, and for a moment the poetics of revelation seems to join hands with the poetics of Revelation. Revelation in fact comes by leaps and degrees to the Dantean persona, it is a strenuous

process, and we may think of the equally fervid and traumatic experience the Stevensian persona undergoes in his search for authentic reality
when we share, in *Paradiso* 1, Dante's shock of exposure to a new order of
reality, which, by its intensity and unbearable radiance, compels the bewildered pilgrim of the Beyond to readjust his powers of perception.
Under Beatrice's stern guidance, a process of heightening purification of
mind gets under way which makes Dante the character shed his earlier
assumptions, engendered as they were by "false imagining":

> Tu stesso ti fai grosso
> col falso imaginar, sì che non vedi
> ciò che vedresti se l'avessi scosso   [1.88–90]

> (You yourself thicken your mind
> with false imagining, so that you fail to see
> what you would see if you had shaken off that veil.)[16]

"Cleanse the doors of perception," as Blake would have put it—an opera-
tion both Dante and Stevens pursue, each in his way.

All over *Paradiso* one feels the cognitive tension that sets Dante's poem
apart from anything his medieval predecessors and contemporaries
wrote. When Beatrice takes over Virgil's tutorial task, she heightens instead of discarding the intellectual function in her loving pupil, who says
of her in *Paradiso* what was to become Galileo's scientific motto:

> Quel sol che pria d'amor mi scaldò il petto,
> di bella verità m'avea scoverto,
> *provando e riprovando*, il dolce aspetto   [3.1–3]

> (That sun who first had warmed my breast with love
> now had disclosed to me the sweet complexion
> Of beautiful truth, *by proving and disproving*.)

Galileo was the arch-dismantler of Dante's beautiful cosmology, but he
appreciated what Stevens was to appreciate in Dante's poetry and poetics: the emphasis on sharp vision, on intellectual experience, and on
cognitive verification, which can lead (as in *Paradiso* 2) to an experimental
attitude. On the other hand, the paradoxically complementary "igno-
rance" Stevens posits as precondition to the rediscovery of reality calls to
mind the childlike state in which Dante repeatedly falls when confronted

by a higher level of revelation in *Paradiso*. The "vital, arrogant, fatal, dominant X" that elicits inadequate metaphors from the human mind is Stevens's decreated equivalent of that divine absolute toward which Dante strives to glimpse it for one overwhelming moment, and to which he keeps calling his language incommensurate.

The search for essence which underlies Dante's poetics in *Paradiso* finds a counterpart in Stevens's idea of "abstraction" as the mark of valid poetry. Dante's focus on ever sharpening vision in the canticle of ultimate Vision parallels Stevens's constant emphasis on the clairvoyant eye. Dante's realist epistemology, in whose terms knowledge happens when the object is present to the unclouded mind, comes very close to Stevens's phenomenology of perception, according to which "description is revelation" and to know is to be, both on the part of the knower and of the known. Perhaps the best illustration of this nonsolipsist principle and of the underlying Dantesque affinity, comes from *The Sail of Ulysses*:

> Under the shape of his sail, Ulysses,
> Symbol of the seeker, crossing by night
> The giant sea, read his own mind.
> He said, "As I know, I am and have
> The right to be." Guiding his boat
> Under the middle stars, he said:
>
> "If knowledge and the thing known are one
> So that to know a man is to be
> That man, to know a place is to be
> That place, and it seems to come to that;
> And if to know one man is to know all
> And if one's sense of a single spot
> Is what one knows of the universe,
> Then knowledge is the only life . . ."   [OP, 99–105]

It does not take a Dante specialist to catch here the obvious cue from *Inferno* 26, where Ulysses describes his breathtaking last voyage into the unknown ocean beyond Gibraltar and in so doing stresses his unquenchable thirst for experience and knowledge. Besides the vast scenery, star studded, Stevens must have particularly liked (and he makes us overhear it in his own impassioned rhetoric) Ulysses' address to his shipmates:

"Compagni," dissi "che per cento milia
perigli siete giunti all'occidente,
a questa tanto picciola vigilia
dei vostri sensi, ch'è del rimanente,
non vogliate negar l'esperienza,
diretro al sol, del mondo sanza gente.
Considerate la vostra semenza:
fatti non foste a viver come bruti
ma per seguir virtute e conoscenza."

("My shipmates," I said, "who through a hundred thousand
dangers made it all the way to the West,
to such a short stretch of your waking life
as now remains, do not deny experience
of the unpeopled world, following the sun.
Consider well the seed from which you came:
you were not made to live like brutes
but to follow the path of valor and knowledge.")

Tennyson acted as intermediary, but Stevens went beyond the late romantic intermediary to the medieval source, if only to turn it polemically around, for here again the modern writer refutes Dante's anthropomorphic theology and restrictive ethics in the very act of valuing Dante's heroic poetry as conveyed in Ulysses' dramatic monologue. Lest anyone doubt that Stevens culled honey from this particular hive hanging in Inferno, let us dwell on Stanza V of *The Sail of Ulysses*, a direct rejoinder to Dante's conception of existence within the framework of a significant consonance:

> We come
> To knowledge when we come to life.
> Yet always there is another life,
> A life beyond this present knowing,
> A life lighter than this present splendor,
> Brighter, perfected and distant away,
> Not to be reached but to be known,
> Not an attainment of the will

But something illogically received,
A divination, a letting down
From loftiness . . .
There is no map of paradise.

The values handed down to Dante by his stern tradition are reversed: unrestrained knowledge of the type Ulysses pursues is no affront to a supreme Deity but the very essence of man's life, and not the road to hell. In so doing, Stevens implicitly shows how much of the "damned" Ulysses there is in the redeemed Dante who ventures beyond the normal thresholds of human experience, downward and upward; and from Dante he takes the idea of paradise as the necessary horizon and stimulus of knowledge, within which something like a secularized Grace descends to our assistance to bless our Ulyssean transgressions. Talking back to Dante in terms of Dante's own myth seems a matchless pleasure to Stevens, who again quotes from Dante's Ulysses in an essay on "The Irrational Element in Poetry": "It is easy to brush aside the irrational with the statement that we are rational beings, *Aristotelians and not brutes* . . ." (italics mine, OP, 218). "Aristotelians" here stands for "followers" of "*virtute e conoscenza*" (virtue and knowledge), the essence of man's terrene dignity as Aristotle's Nicomachean ethics avowedly taught it to Dante himself.

Stevens equates the irrational element in poetry with that incalculable factor which spurs on the creative mind; scholars need the unknown to breathe. Stevens's humanism is not of the rigidly rationalist kind, it incorporates Dante's transcendence in secularized form to hymn "the joy of meaning in design / Wrenched out of chaos," the "beginning of the final order, / The order of man's right to be / As he is," as stanzas 3 and 4 of *The Sail of Ulysses* respectively say. This most impassioned humanist manifesto, which refuses to posit a finite and exhaustible object for man's cognitive drive, has a clearly Faustian ring, unlike the quietist bent apparent elsewhere in Stevens's work. And he achieves this Faustian vision by quoting Dante against Dante, by stealing the ambrosial honey of his remote brother in art from the very dives of hell. Unlike Eliot, who seeks to approach or restore in his own way Dante's transcendent hierarchy of being and values, Wallace Stevens reads Dante with Goethe, Croce, and Santayana in mind, and the result is a fruitful quarrel with Dante. Anchoring man the seeker to this world does not mean to incarcerate him in cramping materialism. Earth incorporates heaven, since heaven ceases to be a reified transcendence to become the necessary horizon of imagination, and reality is, as such, undelusively possessed yet forever to be discovered. Man's own self is the true god and sybil (*The Sail of Ulysses*, stanzas 3 and 8), the creator of all gods, finally intent on going "behind the symbols / To that which they symbolized, away / From the speechfull domes" (*The Sail of Ulysses*, stanza 5). Man's own self is the deepest mystery and the only foundation for knowledge, hence the endless task of "revealing reality" that poetry fulfills in its expanding universe.

That being so, it is easier to understand why Stevens, having said that the great poems of heaven and hell had been written and that the great poem of the earth remained to be written, could also say in *The Figure of the Youth as Virile Poet*:

> . . . if we say that the idea of God is merely a poetic idea, even if the supreme poetic idea, and that our notions of heaven and hell are merely poetry not so called, . . . if we say these things and if we are able to see the poet who achieved God and placed Him in His seat in heaven in all His glory, the poet himself, still in the ecstasy of the poem that completely accomplished his purpose, would have seemed, whether young or old, whether in rags or ceremonial robe, a man who needed what he had created, uttering the hymns of joy that followed his creation. [NR, 51]

It is hard to dismiss the conviction that Dante loomed large in Stevens's mind when he wrote those lines, or these from "A Collect of Philosophy":

> The number of ways of passing between the traditional two fixed points of man's life, that is to say, of passing from the self to God, is fixed only by the limitations of space, which is limitless. The eternal philosopher is the eternal pilgrim on that road. It is difficult to take him seriously when he relies on the evidence of the teeth, the throat and the bowels. Yet in the one poem that is unimpeachably divine, the poem of the ascent into heaven, it is possible to say that there can be no faults, since it is precisely the faults of life that this

poem enables us to leave behind. If the idea of God is the ultimate poetic idea, then the idea of the ascent into heaven is only a little below it. [OP, 193]

The fact that Stevens here is talking of what he takes to be the *itinerarium mentis* of great philosophy, whether theological or secular, and in particular of Schopenhauer, proves once more how deeply rooted the structural and thematic pattern of the *Divine Comedy* was in the American poet's mind; so deeply indeed that it provided him with such a pervasive referential model as to become an archetype for his imagination.

One cannot discuss the intimate nexus between poetry and philosophy in the way Stevens does it here without having Dante's myth in one's bloodstream. If read with the caveat of Santayana's realist humanism, Dante's *Paradiso* would become a parable of man's progress into the plenitude of knowledge and being—a theme not to be invalidated by any accident of historical remoteness or denominational loyalty. Paradise is fullness and fruition, and thus no contradiction subsists between Stevens's high praise for the archetypal "poem of the ascent into heaven" and his statement that what remains to be written is the great poem of the earth. The two poems (or "poems") are aspects of the same theme. In stanza 8 of *The Sail of Ulysses* Stevens says that

> It is the sibyl of the self,
> The self as sibyl, whose diamond,
> Whose chiefest embracing of all wealth
> Is poverty, whose jewel found
> At the exactest center of the earth
> Is need . . .

Unlike Valéry's Jeune Parque, this internalized Muse feeds on indigence and reaches out to the wealth of terrestrial existence; which is another way of saying that poetry, the imagination, springs from an existential need and keeps us alive by its creation of a "heaven" which is no fool's paradise but a viable "supreme fiction" for earth's children.

In all of that, and particularly with regard to Stevens's use of Dante's poetry, George Santayana played a role, even if a late letter by Stevens[17] disclaims any one-sided indebtedness to the "old philosopher in Rome" who elicited from him one of his most moving poems in the early fifties, and who half a century before had confirmed his initiation to poetry in Cambridge, Massachusetts.[18] Perhaps the conclusive testimonial on the matter comes from "A Collect of Philosophy":

> In the case of Santayana, who was an exquisite and memorable poet in the days when he was, also, a young philosopher, the exquisite and memorable way in which he has always said things has given so much delight that we accept what he says as we accept our own civilization. His pages are part of the *douceur de vivre* and do not offer themselves for sensational summary.
>
> Nor are we interested in philosophic poetry, as, for example, the poetry of Lucretius, some of the poetry of Milton and some of the poetry of Pope, and those pages of Wordsworth, which have done so much to strengthen the critics of poetry in their attacks on the poetry of thought . . . [OP, 187]

In the context of a theme which happens to be very germane to both Santayana and Dante, that is, the relationship between poetry and philosophy, no sooner does Stevens bring up Santayana than he thinks of *Three Philosophical Poets*. And at the same time he revises that book's approach by denying the validity of Lucretius, who had won Santayana's approval through the grand endeavor of *De Rerum Natura* to lend a poetical voice to the pioneering naturalism of Democritus and Epicurus. Of the other two philosophical poets selected by Santayana to make up his representative triad, Dante for the Middle Ages and Goethe for the modern age, Stevens says nothing here; he prefers to single out for censure some English masters whose philosophical cerebration does not always result in genuine poetical celebration. The inference suggests itself that Dante's imaginative use of Aristotelian philosophy, no less than Goethe's affinity for a kind of romantic empiricism, ranks high on Stevens's scale of aesthetic value; it is obviously "poetry of thought" like his own, even if Dante's world view involves a scientifically defunct conception of teleological harmony. Dante's specific embodiment of the "poem of the ascent to heaven" does not fall with the demise of Scholastic philosophy. Philosophy itself may formulate a lasting myth, despite the demythologizing bent of philosophers as such. Stevens's relation to Santayana, with whom he shared so much, turns out to be almost as dialectical as his relationship to Dante, with whom he entertained an intermittent but lifelong dialogue that eventually became an argument including in a three-cornered pattern the author of *Three Philosophical Poets*—Stevens's mercurial way of coming to terms with the deep-seated tradition that he made new in his unique manner.

NOTES

1. Holly Stevens, ed., *Letters of Wallace Stevens* (New York: Alfred A. Knopf, 1966), p. 46.

2. Wallace Stevens, *The Collected Poems of Wallace Stevens* (New York: Alfred A. Knopf, 1957), p. 277. Hereafter referred to as CP.

3. Wallace Stevens, *The Necessary Angel: Essays on Reality and the Imagination* (New York: Vintage Books, 1965), p. 23. Part 4 of "The Noble Rider and the Sound of Words." Hereafter referred to as NR.

4. Dante Alighieri, *La Divina Commedia*, G. Vandelli, ed., in *Le Opere di Dante* (Florence: Società Dantesca Italiana, 1960), p. 565 (*Purgatorio* 1.71–72; translation mine). References are to canto and line numbers.

5. Stevens, *Letters*, p. 426. Letter to Henry Church of 28 October 1942: "The fat girl is the earth . . ." For interesting explanations on *Notes Toward a Supreme Fiction* by Stevens himself, see also letter to Hi Simons of 29 March 1943, pp. 443–45. According to Stevens, the "blue woman" in one of the poems of *Notes* refers to the blue sky; and this is an example of how Stevens can create his own anthropomorphic projections of reality to suit the poetical context even while he is dismantling the hardened anthropomorphism of theistic belief, the "pathetic fallacy of God." As he says elsewhere, he can accept belief in a fiction as fiction and as an extension of reality, without taking it at face value when it presents itself as dogma. The imaginary as imaginary is entitled to citizenship in the disabused mind. The pursuit of reality and truth elicits, by contrast, a need for the fictive.

6. Glauco Cambon, "Le 'Notes Toward a Supreme Fiction' di Wallace Stevens," I *Studi Americani* (1955). Now translated as Chapter 3 in *The Inclusive Flame* (Bloomington: Indiana University Press, 1963), pp. 79–119.

7. Ibid., pp. 313–26. Parts I, II, III, and X of this meditative poem, while referring to the figure of the poet as a nameless "he," each time individualize the general idea of the poet as one poet historically placed. Thus the poet of despair conversing with the moon at night on his balcony in a small town is clearly Leopardi, for whom Stevens expressed strong admiration, and the author of "firm

stanzas" hanging "in hell" of Part III is Dante, as I show. Rimbaud might be the figure alluded to in Part X, and Goethe the one in Part I, to judge from the Naples part of his *Italienische Reise*; but some discrepancies compel me to leave the identification in doubt.

8. Samuel French Morse, ed., *Opus Posthumous by Wallace Stevens* (New York: Alfred A. Knopf, 1957), p. 176. Hereafter referred to as *OP*.

9. For Stevens's recognition of Croce's importance as a philosopher of aesthetics, see the letter of 9 January 1941 to Henry Church (*Letters*, pp. 384–85): "But is it possible to discuss aesthetic expression without at least discussing Croce?" Croce's vindication of the imagination as an independent, creative form of knowledge, along with Croce's radically immanent, secular historicism, which among other things led him to read Dante iconoclastically, could only evoke approval on the part of Stevens. Yet Stevens's philosophical bias was much closer to the anti-idealist ontology of Santayana, and Stevens is eloquent about Santayana in his letters, essays, and verse.

10. Stevens, *Opus Posthumous*, "Two or Three Ideas," p. 210.

11. Stevens, *Esthétique du Mal*, in *The Collected Poems*, p. 316.

12. Paul Valéry, *Poésies* (Paris: Gallimard, nrf, 1942), p. 130.

13. Stevens, "The Relations Between Poetry and Painting," in *The Necessary Angel*, pp. 174–75: "Modern reality is a reality of decreation, in which our revelations are not the revelations of belief, but the precious portents of our own powers."

14. I refer in particular to Leopardi's poem, *Alla primavera o delle favole antiche* (To Spring, concerning ancient fables), where he laments the demise of classical myths that gave man a live universe, and also to his *Il tramonto della luna* (Moonset), which depicts the wane of beautiful illusions in the spectacle of the moon's setting below the horizon where the harsh light of the sun will soon burst. In Leopardi's *La Ginestra* (The Broom Flower), man's Stoic facing of a denuded, threatening reality is the theme; and generally speaking, the conflict between fiction (as life-sustaining) and truth (destructively conceived, but finally faced) runs through the whole of Leopardi's prose and verse.

15. Stevens, "A Collect of Philosophy," in *Opus Posthumous*, p. 188.

16. Translation mine.

17. Stevens, Letter to Sister M. Bernetta Quinn of 26 March 1951 in *Letters*, p. 711: "There is an excess, or, rather, a one-sidedness, that spoils them [dissertations on Stevens]. For instance, the writer of The Savage Transparence was purely exegetical. His primary object was to bring Santayana and myself into some sort of relation." See also the letter of 21 July 1953 to Bernard Heringman in which Stevens says of his literary models or sources in general: "I know of no one who has been particularly important to me. My reality-imagination complex is entirely my own even though I see it in others."

18. See, among others, the letter to Jose Rodriguez Feo of 4 January 1945 in *Letters*, pp. 481–82: "I doubt if Santayana was any more isolated at Cambridge than he wished to be. While I did not take any of his courses and never heard him lecture, he invited me to come see him a number of times, and, in that way, I came to know him a little. I read several poems to him and he expressed his own view of the subject of them in a sonnet which he sent me, and which is in one of his books." The editor's note, ibid., adds: "George Santayana, 'Cathedrals by the Sea': Reply to a sonnet beginning 'Cathedrals are not built along the sea,' *A Hermit of Carmel and Other Poems* (New York: Scribner's, 1901), p. 122. Stevens' sonnet 'Cathedrals are not built along the sea' was written on March 12, 1899 . . . and published in *The Harvard Monthly* XXVIII (May 1899), 95." The episode is specifically confirmed in the letter to B. Heringman of 3 May 1949 (*Letters*, p. 637).

WALLACE FOWLIE

Dante and Beckett

At the age of twenty-three, in the year 1929, when he was beginning to participate in the literary life of Paris, Samuel Beckett published an essay entitled *Dante ... Bruno. Vico ... Joyce.*[1] This early text served as introduction to a book written by several authors on Joyce's *Work in progress*, the working title for *Finnegans Wake*, of which the section *Anna Livia Plurabelle* had already appeared in print. Samuel Beckett was at that time collaborating with a few French writers, including Joyce himself, in attempting to translate *Anna Livia Plurabelle* into French. The book of essays or studies on Joyce was called *Our exagmination round his factification for incamination of Work in progress.*

Despite such a title, the twenty pages of Beckett's introduction are the homage of a younger man to an older writer of his day and imply an act of devotion on the part of Beckett and Joyce to Dante as well as to the other named Italian writers: Giordano Bruno and Giambattista Vico. Beckett has clearly demonstrated a lifelong acquaintance with Dante. We might justifiably claim Dante one of the major influences on him, as permanent in his psyche as Proust, Descartes, Arnold Geulincx, and Joyce himself. As well as homage to Dante and Joyce, the early essay of Beckett is an effort to explain Joyce's conception of language. He reminds us that there had been in the fourteenth century attacks on Dante's theory of language in *De Vulgari Eloquentia*, quite similar to those in the twentieth century on Joyce's theory of language.

The opening paragraph is a warning to all literary critics concerning the danger of establishing any neatness of identifications. The final sentence

128

of the paragraph is a call to arms, which the best of our contemporary critics would applaud: "Literary criticism is not bookkeeping." The two authors named at the beginning and at the end of Beckett's title were equally powerful in their mastery of language, although Dante, in using the vernacular, claimed in *De Vulgari Eloquentia* that he wrote a kind of language Italian women spoke in the streets and markets, whereas no creature in heaven or earth, as Beckett says, ever spoke the language of *Work in progress*. Dante, Joyce, Beckett: exceptional linguists, exiles from their native cities, literary artists of the highest importance. All three had acknowledged strong literary masters, writers who served them as examples rather than as creators of forms they imitated. Dante had Virgil and Ovid; Joyce had Homer and Dante and Shakespeare; Beckett had Dante and Joyce.

MALACODA

In a group of thirteen poems, called *Echo's Bones* and written by Beckett between 1931 and 1935, Dante's presence is felt quite distinctly in at least four of the poems.[2] Such a word as "influence" would be inaccurate and inappropriate to call upon in describing this presence. At times Beckett "uses" Dante deliberately and thereby enriches the tone and meaning of his passage—whether it be verse or prose. At other times Dante is an affinity, an echo, almost an atmosphere so native to Beckett that there is no need to distinguish it as a literary or historical atmosphere.

The title *Echo's Bones* is from Book 3 of Ovid's *Metamorphoses*. The word itself, *metamorphosis*, names the strategy employed in the poems, and especially in the poem drawing its name from a demon in the *Inferno*: *Malacoda*. The Ovid text, from which Dante drew frequently in composing his *Commedia*, speaks of the nymph Echo who was rejected by the boy Narcissus. Echo's drama is the loss of love or rather the impossibility of fulfilling the desire for love. All that remains of Echo is her bones and her voice. This is a fate similar to that of Beckett's hero in *L'Innommable* (1953) and to heroes in the works appearing thereafter. In one of Beckett's recent plays, *Pas moi* (*Not I*), the body of the woman speaking is not visible in the play's performance. One sees only her mouth through an opening in the curtain.

In Cantos 21 and 22 of the *Inferno*, we are in the fifth *bolgia* (or ditch) of the eighth circle. There the sinners are punished by demons for barratry, sins against the state and government, for graft and various kinds of dishonesty having to do with money and political positions. We see an assembly of ten demons called Malebranche (evil claws). Their leader is Malacoda (evil tail). At the end of Canto 21, Malacoda leads a procession of devils to direct Dante and Virgil (who without knowing it, are being misdirected). To initiate the start of the procession, Malacoda farts, making a trumpet out of his rump. (It is claimed that this line is the best remembered line in Dante by Italian school boys.) Beckett recalls this detail in his poem and rephrases it in more polite language. He also names one of the Malebranche: Scarmiglione, respelled as Scarmilion.

In Dante, Malacoda is the leader of an infernal procession, both terrifying and comic, that moves through a part of the fifth *bolgia*. In Beckett's poem, Malacoda is an undertaker's assistant who comes three times into a home—presumably Beckett's—in order, first, to take the measurements for a coffin for the deceased husband, and second, to place the body in the coffin, and on the third trip, to cover the coffin. Because Beckett's brief poem is divided into three parts, each based on an action of the undertaker's man, and because Beckett emphasizes this in the opening line:

> Thrice he came
> the undertaker's man

a reader thinks of the three divisions (*le tre cantiche*) of Dante's long poem.

Malacoda is therefore the leader of another kind of procession to the world of the dead. Whereas Dante's procession takes place within that world of the dead although it is organized for a man still living, for the voyager Dante Alighieri, Beckett's procession is organized in this world in order to conduct a man who had died into the other world of eternity. Malacoda (evil tail) presides over the tail end of a life.

Virgil as Dante's guide is puzzled as to how to get from the sixth *bolgia*, and he parleys with the devils for help. Dante, as is often the case, is full of terror. Virgil, more reassured, never forgets that his mission of guide through hell is divinely instituted. Similarly strong sentiments are evident in Beckett's poem in the observant calm of the narrator, who may be the son of the dead man although there is no specific clue to that relationship, and in the grief of the widow whom the narrator wishes to protect from Malacoda, from the coffin-funeral preparations.

The original Virgil, Dante, and Malacoda are all duplicated in Beckett's *Malacoda*. The humor, the scariness, and the solemnity in Dante's Cantos 21 and 22 are present in Beckett's poem. The most notable trait relating the Italian episode to the Irish poem is a deep sense of eeriness and unreality. In Dante, the sufferers are dipped in pitch and clawed by demons. Their human form is mangled and disguised by a viscous covering. In Beckett's poem, the living—the narrator, the mother, and perhaps the undertaker's assistant—are overcome not only by grief but by their momentary proximity to a body no longer totally human. The deceased man in his home is already undergoing a physical change and thereby extending to the living a lesson on human frailty, on the transformation of a body that is the negation of the body, and that will cause the poet to terminate his poem with the monosyllable *nay*. The funeral arrangements would seem to be preparing a voyage, but in reality there will be no voyage, there will be nothing. The one word *nay* is the final line and is detached from the three stanzas. It succinctly negates what the poem builds up in the mind of the reader.

The voyage archetype is the basis of the *Divine Comedy*. It is the primordial structure of the work and one of the explanations for the appeal the poem has exerted through the centuries. The richness, the dramatic intensity, and the endless variety of the episodes in the one hundred cantos are held together and justified by the voyage through the three realms of the other world. *Malacoda* is the earliest text of Beckett's where the voyage archetype is behind the poem's concept but where the impossibility of its achievement is the sense of the poem. For the early characters of Beckett no voyage in the supernatural sense is possible, and for the later characters in his writings—after *Molloy*—there will be no moving ahead, no voyage possible in even the natural sense.

A voyage implies an end, an experience of culmination. Canto 33 of the *Paradiso* is the end of the voyage begun in the *Inferno*, in the opening scene of the *selva oscura*. If, in the writings of Beckett, a voyage is begun or announced, it is never completed. The title itself of *Malacoda* puns on the ending of a life—on the "evil Tail." But the undertaker's man is no devil inhabiting hell and punishing sinners. The last two lines of stanza three:

> all aboard all souls
> half-mast aye aye

unquestionably announce a voyage, but the final long, drawn-out syllable denies the reality of the voyage in which the narrator and the widow would like to believe. The futility of such hope is clearly stated in the final word of the poem—*nay*—contradicting the last two lines, as it will be in the final words of the story *Dante and the Lobster*, and in the final speech of the play *Waiting for Godot*.[3] When the beginning of the voyage is imminent for Dante, in *Inferno* 2, he will doubt his own capacity to undertake it.

> Io non Enëa, io non Paolo sono[4]   [2.32]
>
> (I am not Aeneas, I am not Paul)

But he will never doubt the reality of the voyage.

Each of the three stanzas concentrates on one figure. Stanza one is on the undertaker's man, called Malacoda. The brief stanza two is given to the widow and her mourning. Stanza three is a tribute to the dead man and his hoped-for voyage. Here the tribute would seem to be that of the narrator-son. (Several of the poems in *Echo's Bones* were written soon after the death of Beckett's father, Willie Beckett, in 1933.)

As the original Malacoda and his companion devils, collectively called the Malebranche, supervised the sinners in the afterworld, so the undertaker's assistant in stanza one measures the body for the coffin. This is a real scene, fully recognizable, and yet the assistant is comically disguised behind his bowler hat serving him as a shield:

> impassable behind his scutal bowler.

In the vestibule he appears "knee deep in the lilies," as Malacoda might sink knee deep in the pitch if he fell into it (as some of his fellow devils actually do in the Dantean scene). The assistant is there

> to measure this incorruptible.

In this one theological word *incorruptible* is condensed the reason for funeral preparations in the real world and the reason for the literary allusions to Dante, even if it is the *Inferno*, because all three parts of the *Divine
Comedy* are founded on the belief in the incorruptibility of man. The gross
line associated with Dante's Malacoda is muted in Beckett's, literally
muted in sound, and linguistically muted in an exaggerated choice of
words:

that felts his perineum mutes his signal.

The eternal question of death is raised in the words *must it be*, and
immediately answered and reiterated in the same line:

must it be it must be it must be.

This question and its answer is followed by a beautifully contrived line:

find the weeds engage them in the garden.

The weeds are the widow's dress, and she is to be kept in the garden so
that she may not see what is going on in the vestibule, even if the sound
may reach her.
This note of protectiveness, possibly of the son with regard to his
mother, is the content of stanza two, and is strongly reinforced by the
words:

hear she may see she need not.

To watch the body being placed in the coffin (*to coffin*) would be unbearable for the widow. This is the duty of the assistant. In the second stanza
the name Malacoda is not used, but the descriptive word *ungulata*, referring to hoofed animals, turns him into a devilish form.

to coffin
with assistant ungulata

The third stanza, beginning with the third verb, designating the third
function of Malacoda, *to cover*, terminates the funeral preparations and
speaks a eulogy to the dead man, where a new reference to the fifth *bolgia*
is fused with a transformation of the soul.

The assistant speaks to his assistant:
stay Scarmilion stay stay

which in line 105 of Canto 21 is

"Posa, posa, Scarmiglione!"

Malacoda is asking his assistant to lessen the pain of the closing of the coffin by placing on it a painting of flowers:

lay this Huysum on the box.

This reference to a painting by Huysum as lasting longer than real flowers leads to the principal word of the stanza that has to do with immortality. (Jan van Huysum was a painter of flowers in Holland in the eighteenth century.) It is the word *imago* and is used to replace the dead man:

mind the imago it is he

The image of the deceased will remain in the mind of the narrator (and of the widow) long after the actual death. The perpetuation of the dead is thus assured, as the perpetuation of a flower is assured in a painting. Rarely has Beckett referred to art in this way, although he explained this function of art in his essay on Proust. It might easily be claimed that the poem is the image of the deceased, as the imago, in its scientific sense, is the final state of an insect's life cycle. Imago presents four possibilities: (1) as the permanent picture of natural man, held in the mind of the living, (2) continuing in some other world such as that described by Dante, (3) totally disappearing into a void (*nay*), or (4) undergoing a total metamorphosis (*Echo's Bones*).

From Dante, and from a personal experience, Beckett in *Malacoda* speaks of love and art: of love that is extinguished in the mourning over death and of life that is held in a tenuous altered form in art. Art is therefore an exorcism wresting life out of death, transforming the corruptible (in the vestibule) into something incorruptible. The poem, quite unlike Beckett's earlier poem *Whoroscope*, concentrating on paradox and wit and Descartes's biography, opens the way through its use of Ovid and Dante to the later more profound works. The unreality of the human body, which might be considered the theme behind the themes in *Malacoda*, will continue to obsess Beckett's mind. In most of the subsequent writings he asks in various forms the same question: what can be saved from this unreality? Is the artist the only man able to salvage something from this ambiguity of life leading to death, and of death leading to life, to which Dante's poem testifies?

BELACQUA

In the early collection of ten stories published in 1934 under the title *More pricks than kicks* and reprinted in 1972, Beckett gave to the principal character who appears in all the stories, a name taken from the *Divine Comedy*, that of Belacqua.[5] It is a mysterious name for an Irishman in Dublin in our day, and it has come to represent for most of Beckett's interpreters his strongest and most eloquent relationship with Dante. The opening story, by far the best of the collection, bears the title: *Dante and the Lobster*. After *Malacoda* and other poems in *Echo's Bones* (all written at approximately the same time as the stories), the character of Belacqua is the most obvious clue to Beckett's lifelong interest in Dante.

Before involving Beckett, may we ask and attempt to answer the question: who is Dante's Belacqua? Readers of the *Divine Comedy* know Belacqua is a character Virgil and Dante come upon at the beginning of the *Purgatorio*. Not Purgatory proper, since it is in the fourth canto, but the region usually referred to as ante-Purgatory, that is, the foothills of the mountain.

Prior to the encounter with Belacqua, Dante established a very special mood that penetrates and explains Belacqua, a mood we associate today with the characters of Beckett. It is a nostalgic mood of helplessness and yearning. The souls in ante-Purgatory have not yet sufficiently thrown off their attachment to mortality. Even Virgil and Dante reflect this mood when, in the first canto, they walk along the lonely plain as if they were trying to find a lost road:

> Noi andavam per lo solingo piano,
>   com'om che torna ala perduta strada.   [*Purgatorio* 1.118–19]

> (We were going across the solitary plain,
> Like a man who returns to the road he has lost.)

On reaching a massive boulder in their climb, Dante and Virgil come upon a group of people, of spirits, who are lazily reclining in the shade cast by the rock. They are the negligent ones, the late repentants who must wait out in Purgatory a period of time equal to their time on earth. For having postponed repentance to the last hour, they continue, during their long period of waiting, to appear indolent and, quite literally, to continue knowing the experience of indolence.

Dante has felt fatigue from his difficult climb. Virgil has just explained to him that as they continue the ascent, his weariness will gradually disappear. At that moment Dante hears a voice saying,

> "Forse
> che di sedere in pria avrai distretta."   [Purgatorio 4.98–99]

(Perhaps before then you will have to sit down.)

Dante turns around and sees the people lounging in the shade of the rocky shelf. One of them is sitting alone, aside from the others. By his posture he seems more weary than his fellow spirits. He is clasping his knees and holding his face low down between his knees.

> Ed un di lor, che mi sembiava lasso,
>   sedeva ed abbracciava le ginocchia,
>   tenendo 'l viso giù tra esse basso.   [Purgatorio 4.106–8]

(And one of them, who seemed to me tired,
Was sitting and clasping his knees,
Holding his face down between them.)

Dante is struck by the shade's seeming laziness, and remarks to Virgil that the shade shows himself lazier than if Sloth were his very sister.

The spirit moves his face only slightly over his thigh and says just a few words, but enough for Dante to recognize him.

> Or va tu sù, che se' valente.   [Purgatorio 4.114]

(Now you go up, you who are valiant.)

Dante identifies Belacqua by his brief clipped words and by his lazy posture, and he smiles as he answers his friend from Florence. "Belacqua, I don't need to grieve about you any longer." By these words he means, 'I know you are saved since you are in Purgatory, or ante-Purgatory.' Dante continues with a series of questions both serious and semihumorous: "Why are you seated here? Are you waiting for an escort? or have you simply returned to your old habits?"

We learn at this point that Belacqua, in Florence where he had been a craftsman, a lute maker, was famous for his indolence. The energetic climbing of Virgil and Dante seems ridiculous to him. His posture in ante-Purgatory is one of pious apathy, of comfortable fatalism. In his next words to Dante, which are his last words, he answers succinctly and explains why he is seated and waiting and not actively moving ahead toward his salvation.

> . . . "O frate, andar in sù che porta?
> che non mi lascerebbe ire a' martìri
> l'angel di Dio che siede in su la porta."   [*Purgatorio* 4.127–29]

> ("What use is there of going up?
> God's angel who sits at the gate
> Would not let me pass to the torments.")

Then he explains that because of his delayed repentance, he has to wait out his entire lifetime again.

Belacqua's posture of seeming lethargic waiting is frequent in Beckett, but in Dante's Belacqua there is a valid excuse for the waiting that is absent from Beckett. Dante feels like laughing when he recognizes Belacqua and asks if his friend is back to his old ways. It is a good question and one that might be put to many characters in the *Commedia*. Belacqua's answer is "no!" It has to be "no," because in death, as Dante conceived of it, there is no return, there is always transformation. Death is very infrequent in Beckett. His characters almost never reach it. The two notable exceptions are Belacqua Shuah of *More pricks than kicks*, and Murphy in the novel bearing his name.

In his humor and humanity, Belacqua is as realistically drawn as any character in the *Commedia*. Dante presents his characters by appearance and bearing, as well as by style and tone of voice. In this regard, Belacqua is as memorable as some of the great figures of Hell: Ciacco, Farinata, Brunetto Latini. Little wonder that he has been so important for Beckett. He is in a hunched fetal position concealing as best he can his pathos.

But we must understand that inwardly Belacqua is expectant, knowing that he will eventually enter upon eternity in a different state. Beckett's characters are less expectant or not expectant at all, knowing they are consigned to life that seems to go on forever. But a sense of helplessness in the face of the universe characterizes both Dante's and Beckett's Belacqua. The sound of the name Belacqua is not unlike the sound of the name Beckett. The Irish writer has identified himself in more ways than one with the Dantean character.

Now we may come to the question: who is Beckett's Belacqua as he appears in *Dante and the Lobster* and in the other stories of *More pricks than kicks*?

First, he is a student of Dante. We learn this in the opening sentence of the story. "It was morning and Belacqua was stuck in the first of the *canti* of the moon." (Most exegetes of the *Paradiso* have known a similar experience.) His full name is Belacqua Shuah, so incongruous a name for a Dubliner in our age that we think instinctively of that other contrived name of the Dubliner who preceded him by a few years: Stephen Dedalus. Belacqua Shuah (whose initials are Samuel Beckett's in reverse) is more ridiculous, more clownlike than Stephen, but he is equally bent on learning.

The plot of *Dante and the Lobster* is a day in the life of Belacqua Shuah. It falls into five neatly divided parts: the morning-pondering of the moon spots, lunch which he prepares himself, the lobster he collects for his aunt, his Italian lesson, and the delivery of the lobster to his aunt.

Belacqua has a hard time understanding the moon spots of the *Paradiso*, despite the explanations of Beatrice to Dante. He became "bogged," as Beckett says, and more than that, bored and "impatient to get on to Piccarda." The restlessness over Dante's moon was offset by lunch, which turned out to be a nice affair. Belacqua was strictly alone in preparing it, and that was what he preferred. The flat toaster placed on the flame of the gas ring preoccupied him at some length. The moon spots moved in and out of his mind, as well as episodes connected with the Gorgonzola cheese he was going to eat on the toast. In advance he savored the taste of the lunch, as a kind of rapture as strong as if he were smiting the sledded Polacks on the ice. This reference to *Hamlet* is typical of the bits of learning Belacqua's mind associates with the most commonplace events of his daily life. Ahead of time, he savored his Italian lesson with Signorina Adrianna Ottolenghi. Not only charming, this professoressa was so intelligent that she agreed with him that Italian writers of the nineteenth century, by comparison with Dante, seem like old maids and suffragettes: Manzoni, Pellico, Carducci.

The lobster was ready for Belacqua when he came to pick it up. "Fresh in this morning," said the man who handed it to him. And Belacqua imagined this meant the lobster had recently been killed. But he was anxious to reach the Ottolenghi and begin the Italian lesson.

Belacqua initiated the lesson by laying open to his professoressa the moon enigma. She knew the passage and promised to look it up when she got home. "What a woman!" thought Belacqua. "She would look it up in her big Dante."

Skillfully the signorina moved to a Dantean theme with which she apparently was more familiar, one which indeed is a traditional topic for teachers of the *Divine Comedy*. She referred to Dante's movements of compassion in Hell. Belacqua, an alert pupil, immediately quoted the famous line:

Qui vive la pietà quand è ben morta;   [Inferno 20.28]

(Here pity lives when it is completely dead)

Belacqua spoke of the pun on pietà, meaning both "piety" and "pity" and seemed quite ready to discuss Dante's compassion when he was observing the diviners in Hell. Beckett makes his reader feel that obviously la signorina Ottolenghi was unprepared to cope with such a discussion. The pupil has outdistanced his teacher.

An interruption saved the day for the signorina. The French teacher, Mlle Glain, a neighbor down the hall, had found her cat trying to get into the bag containing the lobster which Belacqua had left in the hallway. She was clutching the cat as she opened the door and asked in great agitation what was in the bag. Belacqua answered "a fish" because he could not remember the French for "lobster," and fish had been good enough for Jesus Christ. The lobster had been saved in the nick of time.

When pupil and teacher returned to the Italian lesson, Beckett writes in a semihumorous, semiphilosophical tone (as he will in later works, with phrases reminiscent of lines in *Waiting for Godot*): "Where were we?" asked Belacqua. "Where are we ever?" cried the Ottolenghi. "Where we were, as we were."

On the last two pages of the story, as a winter dusk falls over the city, Belacqua delivers the lobster to his aunt who is ready in the kitchen with all the necessary paraphernalia to boil it alive.

This final scene unites all the elements of the story. Belacqua sees the lobster moving on the table and cries out, "My God, it's alive what'll we do?" The aunt laughs at him and says: "Boil the beast, what else?" When Belacqua protests: "But it's not dead, you can't boil it like that," the aunt counters with "Lobsters are always boiled alive. They must be. They feel nothing."

Then, in his mind, Belacqua reviews for himself the story of the lobster: how it had crept into the cruel pot in the depths of the sea, how it had survived the assaults of the Frenchwoman's cat in the hallway, and how now it was going alive into scalding water. "Thirty seconds to live," he thought, as the aunt lifted the lobster clear of the table. And then, in just a few words Beckett gives the culmination of the story and underscores its main point.

> Well, thought Belacqua, it's a quick death,
> God help us all.
> It is not.

These three ultimate words, set aside in a paragraph by themselves, seem to mean: "It is not a quick death." In speaking them, Belacqua substitutes for his thoughts on the fate of the lobster, thoughts on the fate of man, and adumbrates in the three words a theme that he will make substantially his own in subsequent works: God's mercy is dubious. This is Belacqua's final comment on the pity-piety line: *Qui vive la pietà.* The lobster, far from resembling a human being, is about to descend into a fiery hell. The aunt in her kitchen is playing the role of Minos who winds his tail around himself and sends the sinner into the appropriate circle. Belacqua's day, which had begun with a reading of Dante's *Paradiso*, ends with a humorous but philosophically stark vision of hell in the kitchen.

It has been pointed out by several critics, and it is important to recall here, that Belacqua Shuah is the first significant incarnation of Samuel Beckett. The resemblances are striking. Belacqua is a poet, a Dubliner, a scholar, a student of Italian, and a lover of Dante. Early in his career, Beckett considered making Italian his central study before he turned to French. Belacqua Shuah is Beckett's first antihero, the first of many, all of whom are characterized, in purely human terms, by failure. The rock under which sits Belacqua the procrastinator below the gates of Purgatory becomes for Belacqua the Dubliner, the tavern, the public house in Lombard Street where he waits for time to pass.

During the course of the ten stories of Beckett, we follow the life story of Belacqua Shuah through three marriages to his death by accident and his burial. At one point in the story *A Wet Night*, he assumes at the very end a posture that seems patterned on Belacqua of canto 4. It is early morning, the rain is falling, Belacqua is drunk, and he is trying to paddle home. His feet pain him so much that he takes off his boots and throws them away. (And of course we think, pedantically inclined as we are, of Estragon's shoes in *Godot*.) He is suffering from such a bellyache that he creeps along "with his poor trunk parallel to the horizon." Finally he collapses and settles into "the knee-and-elbow position on the pavement." It is exactly the posture of Dante's Belacqua:

> sedeva ed abbracciava le ginocchia.

Purgatory is indeed the home of Beckett's characters. Belacqua of the fourth canto knows that his purgatory will come to an end, but the characters of the Dublin writer do not believe that their purgatory will have an end. There is no end to the exploration of self-knowledge, to the examination of the conscious and subconscious selves in Beckett. One admires the heroism of these characters whose waiting has no issue. In time, a mere lifetime, Dante's Belacqua will move up to the angel at Purgatory's gate and be admitted. Beckett's Belacqua and his companions in the other works are plagued by uncertainty and continue their waiting. Only the lobster of the first story is promised a quick death. In that story Belacqua himself, a man who doubts all absolutes including the mercy of God, and all the other characters, the tramps and the cripples of Beckett, wait without knowing what they wait for.

The damned tell Dante very directly and unhesitatingly why they are in Hell and what law they transgressed. And Belacqua in Purgatory tells Dante exactly why he is delayed in his ascent toward Paradise. By comparison with the Dante figures, Beckett's are characterized by vagueness, by ellipses in their speech, by pauses between words, and by silences when they are on the stage. The spirits in Hell have a clear memory of the past, of the time when they were alive. They remember especially those actions that account for the position into which Minos hurled them and which they hold for eternity. Beckett's characters also maintain a connection with the past, but it is veiled and often confused. When the character speaks of himself in the present, he believes—and makes us believe—that he is about to reach the end of his life, that he will continue living only if, as Hamm says in *Endgame*, he can have his painkiller, his *calmant*. As he revives his memories, the past and the present tend to be mingled. Even if they speak as if they have come to the end of their life, Beckett's characters seem to be waiting for something or someone. They seem expectant and thus appear to live in a purgatorial world. The permanency of Hell and Paradise do not figure in Beckett.

Belacqua's mood in Dante is transformed by Beckett into something more serious, into what might be called a meditation of man's fate in this life. As a Beckett character meditates on the uncertainty of life, on the senselessness of life, he often assumes a fetal position comparable to the original Belacqua's and reviews the episodes in his life that have already taken place. The reason for the ceaseless flow of words, for the endless meditations on uncertainty, might well be a belief held by Beckett's characters that there is no possibility of a goal being reached. Between the fourteenth and twentieth centuries, the figure of the Triune God seen by Dante as three concentric circles at the most elevated point of Paradise has changed to an uncertain nondescript and even invisible goal named Godot.

Vladimir and Estragon imagine God to be a figure, perhaps human, perhaps divine, at any rate an anthropomorphic figure. By the end of the play we are certain he will not come to the rendezvous, whoever he is. And we are not certain that he even exists. Neither are the two tramps certain.

More than by the postures of lethargy and suffering, we are held by the personality of Belacqua and by his thoughts on man's mortality. He may be indolent on principle and by temperament, but his successors in the novels and plays hunt for solutions to the problems of mortality.

The name Belacqua returns in Beckett's novel *Murphy*, the structure of which suggests strong parallels with the *Divine Comedy*. The bliss Murphy speaks of is like Belacqua's and would seem to mean the ability to dream through one's life, to discover felicity in a rocking chair. Here is a Belacqua passage:

> It was pleasant to lie dreaming on the shelf
> beside Belacqua, watching the dawn break crooked . . .
> as his body set him free more and more in his mind
> he took to spending less and less time in the
> light . . . and less in the half light, where the
> choice of bliss introduced an element of effort;
> and more and more and more in the dark, in the will-lessness . . .[6]

Murphy's state of *will-lessness*, in his particular definition of bliss, is more reminiscent of the *ignavi* in the vestibule of the *Inferno*, the home of the will-less, of those who made no decisions in life, of Eliot's *hollow men*, than it is of Belacqua in Purgatory, whose position of indolence is dictated as a punishment.

In *Fin de partie* (*Endgame*), Hamm, restricted to his wheelchair, and Clov, in the difficulty with which he walks, are more tormented Belacquas in their inability to reach death.[7] And even in that play we are reminded of the telling phrase in *Dante and the Lobster*: "it is not." Beckett's heroes do not know a quick death. Those three words from the early story apply so precisely to the characters unable to die: the Unnameable, Winnie of *Happy Days*, Krapp listening to his past on tape, that we are inclined to say life is death for Beckett. With Belacqua first, and then with so many of the subsequent heroes, we follow such a rich interplay of distress and wit and compassion that we are, at least momentarily, convinced that the three realms of the *Divine Comedy* exist here on this earth.

GODOT

After the poem *Malacoda* and the story *Dante and the Lobster*, specific allusions to Dante are very infrequent in Beckett's work, but the example and the presence of the Italian writer become more subtle and more significant. It is not at all a question of literary influence in the traditional sense, but rather one of elusive reference and tone and perspective. The real world and the literary world merge in such a memory as Beckett's, and the re-creation his art attempts is unique.

In the *Inferno*, each sinner is condemned to a special kind of torment, in accordance with the law of the *contrapasso*, that of retaliation, which is mentioned only once in the passage on the Provençal poet Bertrand de Born, the schismatic of Canto 28. Whereas Dante's characters are assigned and condemned to a given place forever, the characters in Beckett are condemned to words for as long as they live. They are chained, if we amplify this image, to an implacable need to use words. The words they speak form their principal rapport with reality. Beckett, like every novelist, is possessed by a compulsive need to tell stories. Didi and Gogo speak of this need in them in *Waiting for Godot*. Hamm, in *Endgame*, is writing a novel. Hamm and Clov are obliged to sustain their dialogue as long as they remain in the room that is the set for the play's action. When Hamm says: "Outside, it's death," we understand that he means: 'Outside of words, it's death; when we no longer speak, we will be dead.'

The semidarkness of Belacqua's waiting in the *Purgatorio* is quite similar to the semidarkness of the stage set of *En Attendant Godot*, where the two tramps are seen to move about, at times in considerable agitation, and where two other characters appear and enact a scene in each of the two acts. But the movements of the actors and especially their speeches are efforts to fill the hours of waiting. Their strength is in their waiting, and they move through various phases of comedy, even farce, of pathos, and of ineptness. They are quite literally suffering existence as they live out the history of the self. They tell as much about themselves, in fragments, as Dante's characters do. They review their past as in a primitive rite. They are as firmly in the cast of mortality as Dante's figures are in the cast of immortality.

By now the history of the criticism lavished on the writings of Beckett, the interpretations given to the words in the title *Waiting for Godot*, are almost as numerous and varied as are the interpretations of obscure words and passages in Dante that have been accumulating since the fourteenth century.

In the very first canto, the name *Veltro* plays a role curiously similar to that of *Godot*. Veltro, the greyhound, is obviously the savior of Italy whom

Dante is waiting for. Is he Can Grande della Scala or some other prince whose name might be associated with Veltro and whom Dante may have known? Perhaps he does not yet exist. If he does exist, will he come? We learn the extent of his lands. We learn the need of such a figure for the prosperity of all Italians. And then the action of the poem begins as we enter the first of those realms where the action of a Veltro would not be effective.

The need to believe in a savior—be he political or spiritual—is inherent in man. The necessity to believe in such a figure is more important than his actual coming. Godot does not come in Beckett's play, and the Veltro does not appear in Dante's writings. But Godot is referred to—evasively and obscurely—several times in the play, and Dante refers to a savior-emperor several times in the *Divine Comedy* and in *De Monarchia*, and he dedicates the *Paradiso* to his friend and benefactor Can Grande (whose name means "big dog"). Vladimir and Estragon actually wait for nothing, but they make themselves believe they are waiting for Godot. And Dante, in his hope for a Veltro, demonstrates man's inability to be a nihilist.

There are some slight variations from Act 1 to Act 2 in *Godot*, but no play ever written presents two acts that are so similar one to the other. Time is moving along in *Godot*, but imperceptibly so. The tramps give us the impression of being almost outside of time because the action of waiting never varies. In *Waiting for Godot*, we are practically witnessing the picture of time petrified. In canto after canto of the *Inferno*, we also have the experience of moving outside of time, because we are constantly thrust back into the past, which is relived for us in the speeches of the sufferers. Life is over for the damned, but they wait as they remember the past, and they wait with the full knowledge there will be no change in their waiting.

In referring to Vladimir and Estragon, the French critics universally use the term *clochards*, and American and English critics tend to use "tramps," or, more infrequently, "clowns." As we listen to the dialogue, a relentless game of words like a ball tossed back and forth from court to court, and as we watch the stage, empty save for one prop (a tree, a useful instrument for suicide, and thus referred to in act 2), we have the sensation of watching and hearing two characters, and then four characters, pulled out from the world. If they are not already in hell, undergoing some ingeniously devised torture, they are at least in some intermediary zone between life and death, where life is an hallucination and where death is unattainable.

In the sense of a dramatic performance, Vladimir and Estragon have lost the world, but they have not yet lost the sense of living. They collide with one another on the stage, as they collide with Pozzo and Lucky, in their efforts to appear endlessly busy, and thereby trick themselves into believing that they have not been excluded from the scheme of the world. Francesca, at moments in her narrative, half believes she is still with Paolo in the world, and Capaneo continues in Hell to curse Jove as he had once done on the earth. Hell, for Beckett and Dante, is in truth the futility of action, and therefore those living in hell (or just outside of hell, in a man's mind, for example) have to play at living and pretend they are engaged in human actions. As the sufferers in Dante's Hell know they are damned, so Vladimir and Estragon know they are merely playing, and that is why the two characters of Beckett are best characterized as clowns. Real clowns know they are clowning. They continue to play, night after night, through a sense of vocation, on a strange boundary that stretches between life and make-believe life.

Brunetto Latini, after a moving exchange of words with Dante in Canto 15, has to resume his walk under the flakes of fire in the *girone* of the sodomites, as Vladimir and Estragon have to resume their pose of waiting by the tree after their second meeting with Pozzo and Lucky. They are unable not to wait, as they are unable to leave the bare strip of stage on which they perform no matter who passes by, no matter who is in the audience. If Estragon does leave the stage, it is to go close by and he is pulled back to the stage as to a place where he has to be to exist.

The power of a poem such as Dante's and of a play such as Beckett's is to take a reader and a spectator out of his familiar orientation. The exceptional power of the *Inferno* and *Waiting for Godot* is to create for reader and spectator a total self-estrangement in the world. We find ourselves alienated from our own world although there are recognizable bonds between every canto and the reader's personal world, as there are recognizable bonds between our daily preoccupations and every theme in the dialogues and monologues carried on by the four characters of Beckett.

In the speeches of Farinata and Guido da Montefeltro, despite the immediate settings of the heretics and evil counselors, political events connected with Tuscany and Romagna are recalled, and the moods, memories, and impressions are deliberately sketched in such a way that the past of two strong men is relived.

Farinata appears with Cavalcante Cavalcanti as both Florentines rise up from their burning tombs, and Guido da Montefeltro appears in the same fire that is parted at the top:

> 'n quel foco, che vien sì diviso
> di sopra   [Inferno 25.52–53]

and contains him and Ulysses. In each scene the speech of one sinner gives credence to the speech of the other, and yet we sense there is no beginning and no ending in such scenes. The same absence of a beginning and an ending characterizes the strong alienation effected by Beckett's play. The two Dantean warriors, Farinata and Montefeltro, knew better times and tell us about them, whereas Beckett's clochards give us little indication of a better state from which they have fallen. Inertia prevails in the cases of the estranged tramps, whose moods, thoughts, and emotions are in a constant fluctuation. The very shape of the ideas and emotions and memories of Vladimir and Estragon is forever changing. Whereas a rehearsal of the past is significant and extraordinarily vivid for Dante's characters, such rehearsal for Vladimir and Estragon is merely repetitive and fruitless. The tramps continue to rehearse to one another and continue to tease the audience with themes that almost provide a substantial reasoning: the reference to the two thieves at the crucifixion of Christ, one damned and one saved; the white beard of Godot and the difference between the goatherd and the shepherd. Such brief and undeveloped references to what might be called civilized traditions are diluted in the rising up of unconscious needs and desires. The tramps keep regressing from a civilized tradition to a state that is infernal in its steady repetitiveness.

The concept of time in all of Beckett's work is translated as progress toward death. As the tramps question which day they are living and which particular sentiment they are feeling, they engage in comic routines, devices of repetition that camouflage their distress and move them into metaphysics and even into theology. At moments in the play, they seem to illustrate theological concepts, as Dante's characters stand for given, clearly named misdemeanors. But Beckett's characters are still alive in their hell, and their very waiting for Godot is their principal demonstration of optimism, of the way in which they will overcome mortality. At the beginning of the play, Gogo tells Didi of the closeness he has always felt to Christ: "All my life I've compared myself to him." To reach Christ through playing the clown is a twentieth century routine.

The name of Christ is not mentioned in the *Inferno*. It would be improper for any of the damned, and even for Virgil and Dante, to use the divine name in such a place. The power of Christ's name is such that Vladimir and Estragon use it rarely and prefer to fall back on substitute names: Godot and Pozzo. They wonder if Pozzo, who in the first act is an overbearing figure of authority and cruelty, is Godot, and critics of Beckett's play have raised the same question. The names of the four actors come from four countries, as if from the four parts of the compass and hence from the universe: Russia (Vladimir), France (Estragon), Italy (Pozzo), and England (Lucky).

It is easy to associate Godot with the highest region, with inaccessible heaven. And it is easy, with the help of Dante, to associate Pozzo with the lowest region, with the tragic impotence of the ice region in the ninth circle, at the bottom of which Satan is fixed. In Canto 31, Dante uses twice the word *pozzo*, still today the Italian word for well or pit, to designate the lowest pit of his Hell. The giants surrounding this region of Cocytus first appear to be towers to Dante, but Virgil tells him they are giants and that they are in the pit:

> sappi che non son torri, ma giganti,
> e son nel pozzo . . .   [31–32]

Proper names in Dante—Virgil, Beatrice, Vanni Fucci, Sordello, San Bernardo—have a literal historical meaning as well as a powerful human designation that extends the name beyond itself. Virgil means more than the Latin poet and Beatrice more than a Florentine girl. But in the twentieth century, names have to be mysteriously rewritten and realigned in order to indicate the endlessness of meaning, the innumerable relationships of century with century.

Before appearing in the *Inferno*, Dante's characters had previously lived in history or mythology. Their brief scenes in the poem have made them into mythical creatures for readers today, because they stand not only for themselves as men belonging to an historical period or to a mythological

story, but for some infraction against eternal laws, for a role in life that
was harmful to the city in which they once lived. The name they bear is
so heavy with age that Dante is justified in giving to it designations that
are nonhistorical, that are moral and mythical.

The modern artist rewrites and reforges the name of his character in
order to preserve the mystery of a human life today in its relationship
with the past. History, etymology, and philosophy are used by a Joyce
and an Eliot and a Beckett, as they once were used by Dante Alighieri. So,
the Dubliner Stephen Dedalus is Joyce's hero attempting an escape comparable to that of his mythological ancestors Icarus and Dedalus. Eliot's
Prufrock is Montefeltro, the evil counselor. *Feltro* is *felt* or *filter*, by which a
metal is tested and proved (*Pruf*). And *Monte* is *mount* or *rock*. Eliot, in
presenting his poem, deliberately gave us six lines from Canto 27 in
which Guido da Montefeltro speaks to Dante, as Prufrock speaks to himself (and gives evil counsel to himself). Even the *love song* is in *feltro*, so
close in sound and meaning to *philtre* or the fatal love potion associated
with the Tristan legend.

Godot is Beckett's name, with meanings related to such disparate antecedents as *God* and *shoe* (*godillot*), designating that force which causes men
to "wait." But the power of the play as a whole convinces the spectators
that waiting is synonymous with living and the *clochards* are ourselves; the
play is the picture of life of mankind reduced to its minimum. The waiting in hell is eternal. Each character who speaks to Dante emerges from
his waiting and then we have to imagine his returning to it as Dante and
Virgil move on to the next stage of their descent. If there were more acts
than merely two in *Waiting for Godot*, they would be substantially the same.
Vladimir answers to the name Albert in act 2, and he would probably
answer to other names in succeeding unwritten acts.

The theological concerns of Dante are forever being softened by the
brilliant characterizations he gives, by the settings he provides, by the
dramatic action of each canto. And, in similar fashion, the profound
metaphysical concerns of Beckett are constantly being deemphasized by
the portraits of his antiheroes and their slowed-down actions, by the
pathos and impotence they reveal. The four characters in *Endgame*, the
four in *Godot*, Winnie of *Happy Days*, Krapp listening to his past on tape
recording, Murphy, the Unnameable, and the almost nameless character
Pim of *How it is* (a novel that some scholars argue is a gloss on the *Inferno*)

are heroes facing their fate, but so presented by Beckett that the obstacles they encounter seem ludicrous, so comical in fact that they often seem drawn from circus routines and from the clownings of professional clowns. In following them, it is not hard to forget the great harassments of the human spirit that they all embody.

Through the centuries, some of the most astute commentators of Dante have tried to discover a way out of hell, a hope for an eventual redemption of the damned, indications of a remedial character in the *Inferno*. A few passages, such as Beatrice's speech to Virgil in canto 2, do lend themselves to this unorthodox interpretation, which, if it does have any justification, would lead to a close relationship between the *Inferno* and the *Purgatorio* and even to a joining of the two realms. Characters in the *Inferno* tend to recall events of their lives, significant and guilty events that in the poem explain the eternal condition of the characters. A Beckett character also looks back on his memories (Nagg and Nell in *Endgame* keep recalling a boat ride on Lake Como), but his past and his present tend to be mingled and even confused. And that is why all humanity for Beckett seems to be in a purgatorial rather than an infernal world, because the characters are looking for something and waiting for someone. Even the most pathetic and the most impotent are trying to discover some new awareness of themselves.

Beckett's characters frequently reestimate their status in the world. The opening words of *The Unnameable* represent this rebeginning, this renewed stocktaking: "Where now? Who now?"[8] Because of the very slight degree of hope they contain, such epistemological questions are more purgatorial than infernal. But Beckett's purgatory, if that is an appropriate word, will go on forever. In Beckett's first article on Dante and Joyce (in *Our Exagmination*), he underscores his belief that whereas Dante's *Purgatorio* implies culmination, Joyce's purgatory does not. This same sense of purgatory is Beckett's. His world is in flux: after a sign of progression or advance, there is immediately the antidote, a sign of retrogression or retreat.

Dante presents his characters as having left history in the literally human sense: those in Hell continue to suffer the state of redemption. Beckett presents his characters as men trying to escape from history with its burden of mortality and suffering. Personal traits and biographical data are drastically reduced in a Beckett character. Vladimir and Estragon in the bareness of the stage on which they play, in the vagueness of their memories of the past and in the vagueness of their awareness of the present, resemble clowns. Of all performers the clown is the most humble. In the presence of his public, the clown reenacts gestures and aspirations and defeats that are the most familiar to his public. The *number* of a clown with its sketched caricature of aspiration and defeat, is not unlike a *canto* where a drama unfolds briefly and swiftly.

Whenever an epistemological question occurs in a Beckett work, the critical attentiveness of the character, whether it be the Unnameable or Clov or Vladimir, is so puzzled that the reader or the spectator smiles, as once Dante smiled at Belacqua, at his friend's languorous posture, and the seriousness of the moment—in Canto 4 and in *Godot*—is masked momentarily by the comic. When Beckett exploits the comical-pathetic as Joyce did before him, we realize that he is the most recent writer in Europe—coming after several key writers in the nineteenth century, especially in France (Baudelaire, Mallarmé, Laforgue)—who present the artist as a clown.

It is perhaps in the mysterious word *adventure* where the two Belacquas, separated by six centuries, finally join. *Adventure, ad-venire, avventura*: an experience implying peril, something hazardous, an enterprise of uncertain issue. Such a word neatly characterizes Beckett's ten stories concerned with Belacqua Shuah. Futile adventures they are, because his temperament is basically lethargic. As a prelude to his adventures in *Purgatorio*, Dante encounters the Florentine Belacqua, and smiles at him when he learns that the penitent has to live out again a lifetime of lethargy:

> Li atti suoi pigri e le corte parole
> mosser le labbra mie un poco a riso   [*Purgatorio* 4.121–22]

> (His lazy actions and brief words,
> Moved my lips to smile a little)

Isn't it Apollinaire in *La jolie rousse* who speaks of *l'ordre de l'aventure* as being the order of modern man? Who embarks on such an adventure if it is not the clown, whose acrobatics and stunts are predictably the same each night. He is the one who causes us to smile, whether he be Malacoda, the devil of the fifth *bolgia*, or the undertaker's assistant who uses his bowler hat as a shield, or Estragon trying to pull off his shoe that pains his foot. It is he who in the literal silence of the performing clown leads us to see affinities between the enigmatic replies of *Purgatorio's* Belacqua and the terminal conundrum of Dublin's Belacqua: "*It's a quick death. It is not.*"

NOTES

1. Samuel Beckett, "Dante . . . Bruno. Vico . . Joyce," in *Our Exagmination Round His Factification for Incamination of Work in Progress* (Paris: Shakespeare and Co., 1929). Reissued in New York by New Directions in 1939 and 1962.

2. Samuel Beckett, *Echo's Bones and Other Precipitates* (Paris: Europa Press, 1935). Reissued in *Poems in English* (New York: Grove Press, 1963).

3. Samuel Beckett, *En Attendant Godot* (Paris: Editions de Minuit, 1951); trans. Samuel Beckett (New York: Grove Press, 1954).

4. Charles S. Singleton, ed. and trans., *Dante Alighieri, The Divine Comedy* (Princeton: Princeton University Press, Bollingen Series, 1970). All subsequent citations are from this edition. The translations are my own.

5. Samuel Beckett, *More pricks than kicks* (London: Chatto and Windus, 1934).

6. Samuel Beckett, *Murphy* (New York: Grove Press, 1957), pp. 112–13.

7. Samuel Beckett, *Fin de Partie* (*Endgame*) (Paris: Editions de Minuit, 1957); trans. Samuel Beckett (New York: Grove Press, 1958).

8. Samuel Beckett, *The Unnameable* (New York: Grove Press, 1958).

ROBERT FITZGERALD

Mirroring the *Commedia*
An Appreciation of
Laurence Binyon's Version

I

One brilliant episode of "the Pound era" has fallen into such obscurity as to remain unregistered in Hugh Kenner's book of that title, marvel of registration though the book is. In telling of Ezra Pound's life in London between 1908 and 1920, Kenner refers once or twice to his friendship with Laurence Binyon, poet and Deputy Keeper of Prints and Drawings in the British Museum. But he says nothing of Pound's interest, years later, in Binyon's translation of *The Divine Comedy*. Now, from early in 1934 to late in 1939, this interest animated a great deal of correspondence between the two men and ended with quite remarkable enthusiasm on the part of Pound. In fact, he all but took a hand in the translation. It would be fair to say that he gave as much time and attention to Binyon's work as he had in other years—in another way—to that of James Joyce and for the same reason: that he thought the work was supremely good. Pound could be wildly wrong about some things but not, I think, about a rendering of Dante in English verse. If anyone's ear and judgment had authority in such matters, his did.

Not only has this whole episode been lost to view, but the translation itself is generally and peculiarly disregarded. Teachers of Dante appear to be only dimly aware of it. And yet the rendering of the *Commedia* that most nearly reproduces the total quality of the original poem is surely Laurence Binyon's. Why is it not likely to be supplied to the student or the serious reader of English, either at the University or elsewhere? After puzzling over this state of affairs for some time, I have learned enough to realize that it, too—this relative neglect—is a masterpiece in its way, a *capolavoro* composed by the sheer accidents of history, the fortunes of war and peace.

Here, then, is a story.

II

At Oxford in 1890, Laurence Binyon won the Newdigate Prize with a poem entitled *Persephone*. The year and the title combine to bring us the essential fragrance of a period and to suggest the poetic and scholarly tradition that Binyon inherited. Confining to the sensibility though it had certainly become, that tradition had its points, as Binyon's life would demonstrate. He was a studious poet and a sober man. After Oxford he went to work in the print division of the British Museum, where he was to become a pioneer interpreter of the art of the East to the West, author of *Painting in the Far East* (1908) and later a friend of Charles Freer and Langdon Warner. In 1913 Binyon became Deputy Keeper of Prints and Drawings at the Museum. He and young Ezra Pound met one another from time to time and were notably unaffected by each other's work. Binyon's poems, after all, were in the tradition that Pound proposed to shake. One of them became extremely well known: *To the Fallen*, first printed in the *London Times* in September 1914. This turned out to be so memorable in the English-speaking world that after 1918 many war memorials throughout Britain and the Commonwealth bore a Simonidean stanza from it, cut in stone: "They shall not grow old, as we who are left grow old."

It is worth remembering that in the Print Division Binyon's eye received an education from the masters of line in East and West. He did a great deal of work on Blake. To an eye so educated, no poetry, probably, could match Dante's in visual fascination. Binyon was not an Italian scholar, but as an amateur, with the advice and encouragement of his friend Mario Praz, he began translating *The Divine Comedy*. In 1933 *Inferno* was ready, and late in the year Macmillan published it in one volume with the Italian text on facing pages. The book was dedicated to Praz and carried a brief preface.

The modesty of Binyon's prefatory remarks may have veiled the special nature and ambition of this poem. He had tried, he said, to communicate not only the sense of the words but something of Dante's tone and of the rhythm through which that tone was conveyed. This was not merely a matter of matching, with triple rhyme, Dante's terza rima. It involved a more intimate correspondence. So far as English would permit, and in the decasyllabic line native to English, he had imitated the Dantean hendecasyllable, scanning by syllables rather than feet, but through systematic elisions achieving flexibility in syllable count. The result was a regular but very subtle refreshment and quickening of rhythm, for example, in the *Inferno*:

> "Did ever any of those herein immured
>   By his own or other's merit to bliss get free?"   [4.49–50]

But this was not all, either. By using fine distributions of weight and accent, he had contrived to avoid the beat of pentameters and to even out his stresses on the Italian model. For one conspicuous instance of this he prepared the reader, noting how he had occasionally rhymed on an unaccented syllable (*Inferno* 1.2, "That I had strayed into a dark forest," rhyming with "oppressed")—not intending an abnormal pronunciation, but as "the placing of a heavy or emphatic syllable before the final word seems to have the effect of mitigating the accent on that word, so that it is rather balanced between the two syllables than placed with all its weight on one. Such elasticity of stress seems congenial to Dante's verse." No doubt Binyon learned the possibility of this, and the advantage of it, from Dante Gabriel Rossetti, who had resorted to it here and there in his translations of Dante's sonnets and *canzoni* in the *Vita Nuova*.

But Binyon went far beyond Rossetti, as he had to, in working out a style adequate to the *Commedia*—a style versatile but consistent, firm, but well wrought and swift. Drawing on the English of earlier centuries, he would admit old forms and words, but with a selective and measuring ear so that his archaisms generally gave body and life to his verses, not quaintness. The diction, thus slightly expanded and elevated, was an accomplishment in itself. It stood, in fact, to twentieth century English very much as Dante's living Tuscan does to twentieth century Italian. One brief example may suffice:

> As runneth up before the burning flame
>   On paper, a brown colour, not yet black,
>   And the white dieth, such their hues became.   [Inferno 25.64–66]

Binyon's Inferno was published, as I have said, late in 1933. The editor of the Criterion in London, at Ezra Pound's request, sent this book to Pound for review. Pound was then living in Rapallo; he had left London thirteen years before, and he had not spent the interval extolling the English literary establishment, to which Binyon in a quiet way belonged. But a foolish note on Binyon's translation had fallen under his eye and aroused his curiosity. The editor of the Criterion must have awaited Pound's review with several kinds of interest. The review appeared in April 1934.

> I state that I have read the work, that for thirty years it never would have occurred to me that it would be possible to read a translation of the Inferno from cover to cover, and that this translation has therefore one DEMONSTRATED dimension. . . . The venerable Binyon has, I am glad to say, produced the most interesting English version of Dante that I have seen or expect to see. . . .
>
> The younger generation may have forgotten Binyon's sad youth, poisoned in the cradle by the abominable dogbiscuit of Milton's rhetoric. . . . At any rate, Dante has cured him. If ever demonstration be needed of the virtues of having a good model instead of a rhetorical bustuous rumpus, the life in Binyon's translation can prove it to next century's schoolboys. . . . He has carefully preserved all the faults of his original. This in the circumstances is the most useful thing he could have done.

What these faults were the reviewer did not expressly say, but it became clear that he meant inversions of word order. Unspeakable syntax had been a bête noire to Pound since the days of imagism, and he now found himself irritated by "Binyon's writing his lines hind side before." But on reflection he had come round to seeing that some of this was appropriate.

The devil of translating medieval poetry into English is that it is very hard to decide HOW you are to render work done with one set of criteria in a language NOW subject to different criteria. . . . The concept of word order in uninflected or very little inflected language had not developed to anything like twentieth century straightness.

When the reviewer got down to cases, his technical observations were as acute as might have been expected.

Working on a decent basis, Binyon has got rid of magniloquence, of puffed words, I don't remember a single decorative or rhetorical word in his first ten cantos. There are vast numbers of monosyllables, little words. Here a hint from the *De Eloquio* may have put him on the trail. In the matter of rhyme, nearly everyone knows that Dante's rhymes are "feminine," i.e. accent on the penultimate, *crucciata, aguzza, volge, maligno*. There are feminine rhymes in English, there are ENOUGH, possibly, to fill the needs of an almost literal version of the *Divina Commedia*, but they are of the wrong quality: *bloweth, knowing, wasteth*. Binyon has very intelligently avoided a mere pseudo or obvious similarity, in favour of a fundamental, namely the sharp clear quality of the original SOUND as a whole. His *past, admits, checked, kinds*, [are] all masculine endings, but all having a residue of vowel sound in state of potential, or latent, as considered by Dante himself in his remarks on troubadour verse.

The fact that this idiom, which was never spoken on sea or land, is NOT fit for use in the new poetry of 1933–4 does not mean that it is unfit for use in a translation of a poem produced in 1321. . . . Coming back to the rhyming, not only are we without strict English equivalents for terminal sounds like *ferrigno, rintoppa, argento, tronca, stagna, feruto*, but any attempt at ornamental rhyme à la Hudibras, or slick epigrammatic rhyme à la Pope or trick rhyme à la Hood, or in fact any kind of rhyming excrescence or ornament would be out of place in the *Commedia*. . . .

One ends with gratitude for [the] demonstration that forty years' honest work do, after all, count for something; that some qualities of writing cannot be attained simply by clever faking, young muscles or a desire to get somewhere in a hurry. The lines move to their end, that is, draw along the eye of the reader, instead of cradling him in a hammock. The main import is not sacrificed to detail. Simple as this appears in bald statement, it takes time to learn how to achieve it.[1]

These remarks seem to be valuable above all in that they shed a shrewd—and unique—craftsman's light on the art of The Divine Comedy and the task of translating it. Pound obviously felt enticed by the challenge that Binyon had taken up—so much so that he could not stay on the sidelines. In the course of preparing his review, he wrote to Binyon on 21 January 1934.

My dear Laurence Binyon: If any residuum of annoyance remain in yr. mind because of the extremely active nature of the undersigned (it is very difficult for a man to believe anything hard enough for it to matter a damn what he believes, without causing annoyance to others)—anyhow. . . . I hope you will forget it long enough to permit me to express my very solid appreciation of yr. translation of the Inferno. Criterion has asked me for a thousand words by the end of next week, but I am holding out for more space [he got six thousand] which will probably delay publication for heaven knows how long. When and if the review appears and if it strikes you as sufficiently intelligent, I shd. be glad thereafter to send you the rest of the notes I have made. Minutiae, too trifling to print. But at any rate I have gone through the book, I shd. think, syllable by syllable. And as Bridges and Leaf are no longer on the scene, the number of readers possessed of any criteria (however heretical) for the writing of English verse and at the same time knowing the difference between Dante and Dunhill is limited. . . . I was irritated by the inversions during the first 8 or 10 cantos, but having finished the book, I think you have in every (almost every) case chosen the lesser evil in dilemma. For 40 pages I wanted you to revise, after that I wanted you to go on with the Purgatorio and Paradiso before turning back to the black air. And I hope you will. I hope you are surviving the New England winter. . . .[2]

Binyon was surviving it very well. At sixty-five he had retired from his job at the British Museum and had gone to Cambridge, Massachusetts, for the academic year to give the Norton Lectures—he followed Eliot in that chair—lecturing not on poetry but on oriental art. He replied from the Commander Hotel on 18 February 1934:

> My dear Ezra Pound, I was very glad to hear from you, and to learn that you had read my Inferno version with so much interest. The difficulties are so immense—often I was in absolute despair—that after surmounting them in a way that didn't seem too bad one was inclined to rate the feat too highly: now, when I turn the pages again a lot of it seems terribly inadequate. (Of course *all of it* is inadequate; that goes without saying; but some passages read well, I think, at any rate apart from the Italian.) When you say "inversions," do you mean grammatical inversions or inversions of accent? I shall see when your review appears, if it does appear, as I hope. I shall certainly be very glad of your notes, as I know one can go on improving forever in the matter of details. Shall I go on with the Purgatory and Paradise? I don't know. It takes a devilish amount of time and hard work, but I have done I think 8 cantos of Purgatory so hope to finish that some day. We are having the severest winter on record in the States, but are surviving without any frost-bitten members so far. The bright sun is welcome after grey London, which I have now left for good. . . .[3]

So ran the first exchange—friendly if a trifle wary on the part of both men (I hear a reticent gesture of *rapprochement* in Binyon's last remark about London). This led to four or five other exchanges in the course of 1934. Pound's letters were copious and high-spirited, Binyon's briefer and plainer; every now and then he would patiently maintain a point. He enjoyed the *Criterion* review which he found waiting for him in June on his return to England and to his retirement farmhouse in Berkshire. He wrote to say that he felt encouraged and grateful, and venerable though he might be he had lots of energy left and hoped to go on. Pound reported in June: "Yeats rumbled in last week / also agreed that you had done a damn good job (my phrase, not his) . . . he assented with noble dignity."[4] As he had promised, Pound sent Binyon his review copy of the book with marginal notations, which Binyon recorded gratefully before returning the book in July. "Of course," he wrote, "in many places you pounce on [things] I should vastly have preferred to be quite plain and direct, but it is devilish hard to get the rhyme, at the same time—as you know. In fact, sometimes impossible. However, you have noted a number of lines wh. I shall try to improve."

In August Binyon wrote to thank Pound for sending him a copy of the Cavalcanti Rime in Pound's edition. He said: "I quite see that the having music in view was a gain to the lyric of Campion, etc., necessitating clearness, lightness, a clear contour. But it seems to me that you couldn't go on forever within those limits: and I don't see that the alternative is necessarily 'rhetorical declamation.' Poetry to me is a kind of heavenly speech." As though by tacit agreement, neither man ever mentioned what each knew the other had in mind: the poetry of Milton. In November Binyon sent Pound versions of the first cantos of the Purgatorio. At the end of January 1935, he added a few more and said that at Eliot's request he had sent the Sordello canto (5) to the Criterion. Then he went off to Egypt to lecture. Pound continued to think the work over. On the 29th of April he concluded a letter (the last in this series):

> When you get the Paradiso done the edition shd. go into use in all university Dante study; at least in America. I don't know WHAT study is committed in England . . . possibly Dante is still considered an exotic. Temple edtn/ was used in my undergrad/ time, but yours sheds so infinitely much more light. . . . And as translation, I don't mean merely of Dante, but in proportion to any translation I can think of, I don't know of any that is more transparent in sense that reader sees the original through it. A translation that really has a critical value, i.e. enlightens one as to the nature of the original. That is rarissima. I don't think my own DO. I have emphasized or dragged into light certain things that matter (to me at any rate) but it is not the same thing. . . . I shall probably do a note on the Purg in Broletto [a new monthly magazine published at Como].[5]

After this there was a long hiatus in correspondence. It was nearly 3 years later, 25 February 1938, when Binyon wrote again. "I imagine you will be thinking me extinct," he said. "I have at last finished the Purgatorio, and it has gone to the printer. I didn't want to bother you with bits at casual intervals but I wonder if you would care to look through proofs of the whole?" Pound agreed at once. Late in April the proofs were sent. Pound's letters with detailed comments now came thick and fast, more than half a dozen long letters on batches of cantos between April 22 and May 12.

Binyon had cautioned him: "But don't take too much trouble now; because, as my Inferno was a complete failure from the sales point of view and Macmillan lost over 200 over it, I can't expect them to pay for a heavy lot of corrections, nor can I afford to pay myself." This had not the slightest effect on Pound. Typical of Poundian comments gratefully received and acted on were his remarks on 11.86–87, *gran disio del eccellenza*, as to which he wrote: "'desire of excelling or beating someone else' is the meaning, not the 'desire of perfection,' Our 'excellence' is almost a synonym with 'goodness,' As the whole poem is one of fine moral distinctions, this dissociation is worth making."[6]

Wrote Binyon on 27 April: "What I have aimed at above all is getting something like Dante's 'tone of voice,' and my Italian critics and Italian friends all think this is the chief merit of my version. It is the first thing they say. (The English ones say terza rima is un-English, etc.)" Pound's enthusiasm mounted as he read. After Canto 17 he wrote: "MAGNIFICENT FINISH! Utterly confounds the apes who told you terza rima isn't English. . . . The beauty here would only have been got by using terza rima. Lascia dir gli stolti who don't see it and who have been for two centuries content that *technique* went out of English metric with Campion and Waller." At Canto 21 he exclaimed, "Banzai, my dear BinBin," and at 28, "Bravo, Bravo, Bravo."

We might listen to a passage from that Canto, 28: the narrator's account of his meeting with Matilda in the *paradiso terrestre*:

> Already my slow steps had borne me on
>   So far within that immemorial wood
>   That I could no more see whence I had gone;
> And lo! a stream that stopped me where I stood;
>   And at the left the ripple in its train
>   Moved on the bank the grasses where it flowed.
> All waters here that are most pure from stain
>   Would qualified with some immixture seem

Compared with this, which veils not the least grain,
Altho' so dark, dark goes the gliding stream
   Under the eternal shadow, that hides fast
   Forever there the sun's and the moon's beam.
With my feet halting, with my eyes I passed
   That brook, for the regaling of my sight
   With the fresh blossoms in their full contrast,
And then appeared (as in a sudden light)
   Something appears which from astonishment
   Puts suddenly all other thoughts to flight)
A lady who all alone and singing went,
   And as she sang plucked flowers that numberless
   All round about her path their colours blent.
"I pray thee, O lovely Lady, if, as I guess,
   Thou warm'st thee at the radiance of Love's fire,—
   For looks are wont to be the heart's witness,—
I pray thee toward this water to draw near
   So far," said I to her, "while thou dost sing,
   That with my understanding I may hear.
Thou puttest me in remembrance of what thing
   Proserpine was, and where, when by mischance
   Her mother lost her, and she lost the spring." [Purgatorio 28.22–51]

The reader of severe contemporary taste and habituated to contemporary style may find this idiom—one, as Pound put it, "never spoken on sea or land"—at first glance an exercise in the antiquarian. But he will be aware of its clearness and fluency, and as he reads on he will, I believe, begin to feel, as Pound did, the distinction of its fashioning as a medium for the great medieval poem. This cumulative effect cannot be conveyed by quotation, but from the quoted passage the reader may gain an inkling of the means employed. One may notice, for example, in the third tercet the limpid monosyllables of the enclosing lines and the cunning "immixture" of polysyllables in the line enclosed. The fourth tercet is a good one in which to sense the evenness that Binyon achieved in weight of syllables, like musical notes, an effect twice assisted on this page by a flattening out of the rhyme word ("contrast" and "witness"). In the final tercet one may hearken not only to subdued alliteration ("puttest," "Proserpine," "mischance," "mother") but to covert internal rhyming ("hear," "where," "her"). Every one of these refinements is a resemblance to the Italian. So controlled and sustained is Binyon's artifice, and so free of any kind of flashiness, that it acquires a life of its own, and this life in the end seems very nearly the life of the original.

In Canto 32 Pound came upon what he called "the only line of really bad poetry I have found. . . . 'But when she rolled on me her lustful eye' might be Gilbert and Sullivan. Positively the only line that is out of the sober idiom of the whole of your translation. Like Omerus he SLEPT. Moderate verb and adjective wanted." (Binyon toned it down.) At the end Pound wrote: "Once again my thanks for the translation. And there are damned few pieces of writing that I am thankful for. . . . Nobody has had such a good time of this kind since Landor did his notes on Catullus. . . . And now, Boss, you get RIGHT ALONG with that Paradiso as soon as you've stacked up the dinner dishes."

Binyon's *Purgatorio* was published in September, with an acknowledgement of Pound's assistance. As he had promised to do three years before, Pound wrote a notice of the book in Italian for *Broletto*. This article has to my knowledge never been translated and has remained forgotten or unknown. Yet it expressed a serious and long-meditated judgment, without reserve. It was headed: "BINYON: We greet a most valuable translation of the Divine Comedy," and proceeded (my translation):

> I can repeat all the praises published in *The Criterion* when the translation of the *Inferno* appeared; but I must add still others. Constantly developing his technique, Binyon in his description of the Terrestrial Paradise reaches a true splendor and clarity never achieved before. It seems to me that this can be said not only in comparison with the other translations of Dante, but perhaps also in comparison with the whole body of translations into English of any author whatever. . . .

What about Golding's *Ovid* and Douglas's *Aeneid*, old favorites of Pound? These were, he observed, works of poetry that had no need of the originals and served not as interpretations of the originals but as comment of a special kind.

Binyon [he said] triumphs in another way, he triumphs through an honesty that from time to time amounts to genius. His version of Dante gives me a clearer sense of the original. It is like a window with glass so polished that one is not aware of it, one has the impression of the open air. . . .

My generation in America suffered from the assumption that to understand Dante it was necessary to suffocate in a pile of commentary. I, at least, at seventeen was distracted by the abundance of comments and notes and sometimes lost the continuity of the poem. With a prose "argument" of half a page or less for each Canto, Binyon has very clearly shown the falsity of this assumption. . . .

As for *terza rima*, Binyon achieves beauties that he could never have attained except by making the effort to employ this form, in which he gets a very English flavor with words like *coppices*, or *highlander* for *montanaro*. . . .

The defects of his version are superficial. I see none except in little inversions, which could easily disappear in a revision which the translator already intends to make as soon as he has finished the whole version of the poem. Some defects have already disappeared between the first proofs and those passed for the printer. . . .

But undoubtedly Binyon has already made us a triple gift. First true poetry, in his most felicitous pages. Second: a sense of the continuity and comprehensibility of the poem. Third: as assistance to students . . . every class for the study of Italian poetry in any foreign university ought to make use of this version to facilitate the comprehension of the *Commedia*.

A decadence begins when attention turns to the ornamental element and is detached little by little from the meaning. In Dante (and in Guido) the meaning is extremely precise; if you doubt it, look at Canto XVIII of the *Purgatorio*. The idiom of Binyon's version is the idiom suitable for translating a poet to whom meaning was far more important than ornament. The defects are like nutshells on the table after a magnificent meal.[7]

III

I digress from my story a little, but I'll return to it. The grace of God came to Dante in many forms but in none happier for his poem than the terza rima. It was a miraculous formal invention or *trouvaille*. As the formulaic hexameter buoyed and carried the Homeric singer, so the terza rima collaborated (it is not too much to say) in the making of the *Commedia*. It gave Dante what he needed for his narrative, a flexible unit beyond the line, capacious enough for description and figure, argument and speech, capable of endless varieties of internal organization, and yet so compact as to make for the famous concision; above all, through the ever-developing rhyme scheme, it gave him continuous movement forward. Terza rima is a formal paradigm of Aristotelian Becoming—the latent or "virtual" thing constantly coming into actuality, as each new tercet fulfills with enclosing rhyme the rhyme enclosed in the preceding one. The lyric tercet, moreover, conduced to the design of the poem in cantos or songs of lyric length (the average length in fact nearly conforms to Poe's limit for lyric, reckoned five hundred years after Dante). For these reasons and others, the life of the *Commedia* is inseparable from its forms, and a prose rendering alters the nature of the animal even more drastically than usual. Implicit acknowledgement of this is made in the Temple Classics version where the Carlyle-Okey-Wicksteed prose is printed in units or versicles corresponding to Dante's tercets.

The "transparency" valued by Pound in Binyon's version was therefore a formal achievement: Binyon had emulated and matched in English the labor of the original poet in Italian, so that the reader could see through the movement of the English poem the movement of the original composer's invention, working in verse and in verse of just this kind. Of just this kind? Yes, insofar as the Italian hendecasyllable can be matched by decasyllabic lines in English. And in fact the one is closer to the other than may superficially appear. It is close historically, because Chaucer wrote his heroic line with continental syllabic verse, in particular Dante's Italian, in his ear (he was Dante's first translator), and easily every third line in Chaucer is hendecasyllabic because of the nature of Middle English. It is close rhythmically, by virtue of the phenomenon noted by Pound: that in many a masculine ending in English the terminal consonant will carry a latent following vowel sound similar at least to the semi-syllable of "e muet" if not to the Italian full vowel. The poet and scholar, F. T. Prince, has been able to argue that it was from the Italian hendeca-syllable that Milton derived his line in Paradise Lost,[8] and Binyon in turn derived his system of elision from Milton as analyzed by Robert Bridges. By the device he pointed out in his preface and by other subtle means, he gave his lines the metrical character of the lightly running Italian.

Now twenty years of work on Binyon's part and nearly six years of attentive participation by Ezra Pound led up to nothing less than the miseries and oblivions of the Second Great War. After sending drafts of the first Paradiso cantos to Pound and writing to him on 29 December 1939, Laurence Binyon never heard again from his friend in Rapallo. The correspondence they had already had remained in their respective files. No English translation of Pound's Broletto article appeared, or was to ap-pear until this writing. Binyon kept his pad on his knee in the wartime evenings; he finished his Paradiso. Macmillan published it in 1943. On March 10 of that year Laurence Binyon died in a nursing home in Read-ing, and his obituary appeared next day in the London Times. Along with it appeared news of the Russian armies defending Kharkov and the latest R.A.F. raid on Germany—five hundred tons on Munich. It was not a good year for Italian studies. If Macmillan had lost money on Binyon's Inferno, it certainly did not make any on his Purgatorio and Paradiso. Indeed, all three volumes were allowed to go out of print for long periods and have almost never been in print at the same time.

So matters stood when the war ended in 1945. What trouble had come upon Ezra Pound it is hardly necessary to recall; few people knew or would know for years of his admiration for Binyon's Dante or the rea-sons for it. Some Dantisti remained aware of the Binyon translation. When Paolo Milano edited a Portable Dante for Viking in 1947, Macmillan, for a courtesy fee, allowed him to include Binyon's entire Divine Comedy. "Binyon," wrote Milano, "never distorts the original style; he never takes us beyond the range of Dante's own voice." But Binyon's preface, with its clues as to how this great virtue had been worked for, did not appear, nor was it quoted, in the Viking Portable.

W. H. Auden reviewed this book briefly but appreciatively in the New York Times; so did Louise Bogan in the New Yorker. In the United States the portable sold moderately for a while (bringing nothing, courtesy of Mac-millan, to the Binyon heirs), and moderately, again, in a paperback edition (1955), but there was no counterpart in England during the 1940s. In those years, however, Penguin Books began to bring out, as "Penguin Classics" under the general editorship of E. V. Rieu, paperback translations, like Rieu's *Odyssey*, priced within range of the railway bookstall trade. For the Penguin Dante, the translator selected was Dorothy Leigh Sayers, and her *Hell* was published in 1949.

It was a formidable work. She, too, had done the poem in English terza rima. She quoted Binyon's friend Maurice Hewlett as saying that for the translator of Dante it was "terza rima or nothing." With Anglo-Catholic ardor and intellectual bounce, the author of *Gaudy Night* and *The Nine Tailors* provided a long introduction, extremely full notes, and a glossary. In her time Dorothy Sayers had won a first in medieval literature at Somerville College, Oxford, and she wrote with professional skill. Her *Hell* caught on and has been reprinted practically every year. She followed it with a Penguin *Purgatory* in 1955, and after her death in 1957 her friend Barbara Reynolds, general editor of the *Cambridge Italian Dictionary*, added the concluding dozen or so cantos of *Paradise* for publication in 1962. *Purgatory* and *Paradise* have been reprinted many times. All are to be found in university book stores in the United States.

One result of these estimable works, however, was not fortunate. If Macmillan had ever intended in the fullness of time to venture a new printing of Binyon's *Divine Comedy*, in the edition with Italian and English on facing pages, the currency of the Sayers version in inexpensive Penguins must have made such a venture seem quixotic. In 1965, in fact, when the question arose, Macmillan pondered a new printing and decided against it. One further development has probably ruled out the possibility forever. In 1972, Chatto and Windus brought out the Viking *Portable Dante* in England, retitled *Dante: The Selected Works*. Remarkably enough, Binyon's name appears neither on the cover nor on the title page of this book, but his version of *The Divine Comedy* is now in print in this form (again minus the preface) in the United Kingdom. Neither there nor in the United States can you buy the bilingual edition that Pound thought should supplant the Temple Classics edition for the undergraduate study of Dante, and the chances are heavily against undergraduates or anyone else ever having it.

This being the case, and admitting the seriousness and utility of Dorothy Sayers's presentation, the quality of her translation, which has already represented the poetry of Dante to several generations of students, invites a little study. When she undertook her work, she was apparently unaware of Pound's *Criterion* review of Binyon's *Inferno*, nor could she have known of the Pound-Binyon correspondence, since none of it appeared in print until eight of Pound's letters were published by D. D. Paige in *The Letters of Ezra Pound* in 1950. If thereafter she became aware of this material, she gave no indication of it in her *Purgatory* or *Paradise*. This may or may not have been to her advantage. Consider the question of feminine rhyming in imitation of the Italian hendecasyllabic line.

"I have used a liberal admixture of feminine rhyme," she wrote in her first introduction. "This is the usual English custom, and I do not know why Dante's translators for the most part fight shy of it." It was perhaps an understandable perplexity, but it had already been resolved by Binyon and Pound. Even without benefit of that solution, the translator might have reflected that a *liberal* admixture of lines that differ in termination from the norm is not like Dante's practice. His *versi tronchi* (accent on the ultima) and *versi sdruccioli* (accent on the antepenult) are rare and exceptional. But once her decision was taken, Sayers went vigorously ahead and allowed herself a good deal of the rhyming "excrescence" that Pound thought out of place in the *Commedia*. At the opening of *Inferno* 22, for example, she composed four successive tercets with nothing but feminine rhymes and in the fifth added a flourish of the *sdrucciolo* type. It is true that in the Italian of this passage there are subtle irregularities of accent, but the effect of the Sayers English is to carry these to the point of burlesque—and what is true of this passage is true of all too many others.

One might argue that variety of this kind, not only in meter and rhyming but in diction as well (she did the Provençal of Arnaut in *Purgatorio* 26 in Border Scots) make the Sayers translation more readable and save it from monotony. That may be true in this sense: clearheaded and ingenious as she was, but endowed with limited gifts as an English poet or stylist, Dorothy Sayers did well to conceive her work in a way that would utilize her strengths. Her translation is not often dull and is almost always clear—at times clearer than Binyon's. Let one example suffice:

> Così fatta, mi disse: 'Il mondo m'ebbe
>   giù poco tempo; e se più fosse stato,
>   molto sarà di mal, che non sarebbe. . . .   [*Paradiso* 8.49–51]

Binyon:

> Transfigured thus, it spoke: 'The world below
>   Held me not long; and much would not have happed,
>   Had it been longer, that now comes in woe. . . .

Sayers:

> And shining thus he said: "The earthly scene
>   Held me not long; had more time been allowed
>   Much ill that now shall happen had not been. . . .

With her command of workmanlike English and her chosen latitude in rendering, she managed often enough, as in this case, to avoid the "faults of the original"—and of Binyon—in the matter of inverted word order. Without reference to the Italian, as an extended work converting Dante tercet by tercet into English verse, her *Comedy* is a considerable achievement.

Binyon's is simply an achievement of a higher order. His taste is finer. He does not indulge those bright ideas that confuse everything. His style is distinguished and steady, as for all its resources of idiom and invention one feels Dante's style to be. He had indeed caught Dante's "tone of voice." His or any English must be more humid than the dry burning Italian, more muted in sonority, less Latinate and closely knit. But line by line he represents his original with that honesty amounting to genius that Pound remarked. In order fairly to support this judgment, let me examine in both versions a passage of some length, at a point in the poem where each translator after much practice may be supposed capable of his best—the opening of the *Paradiso*.

> La gloria di colui che tutto move
>   per l'universo penetra e risplende
>   in una parte più e meno altrove.   [1.1-3]

Sayers:

> The glory of Him who moves all things soe'er
>   Impenetrates the universe, and bright
>   The splendour burns, more here and lesser there.

Occurring at the end of the first line, "soe'er" could not be a more no-
ticeable archaism. It is also an addition to what the Italian says, and it
concludes the line with a double sibilance following the plural "things."
No less conspicuous in another way is "impenetrates" in line 2, an un-
common word that seems tautological rather than intensive; in fact, as it
adds nothing to the idea of penetration, it seems forced. In line 3, the
verb "burns" goes beyond the Italian, and does so emphatically through
the position of the verb at the point of caesura.
Binyon:

> The glory of Him who moveth all that is
>   Pervades the Universe, and glows more bright
>   In the one region, and in another less.

Here there is archaism in the old form, "moveth," but the word occurs
midline and is compact, not fluttery. It serves to avoid sibilance, and it
reproduces the dissyllabic Italian *move*. "All that is" preserves the singular
of the Italian *tutto*. In line 2, "pervades" is the right word to render penetration by light, and the three syllables of "glows more bright" follow the
contour of *risplende*. Getting in the comparative in this line not only accords with English idiom but makes it easy for the next line to retain the
chiastic order of the Italian, "more . . . in the one region . . . in another
. . . less." Moreover, the word *parte* is translated here, as it is not by Sayers.

> Nel ciel che più della sua luce prende
>   fu'io, e vidi cose che ridire
>   né sa né può chi da là sù discende;   [1.4–6]

Sayers:

> Within that heav'n which most receives His light
>   Was I, and saw such things as man nor knows
>   Nor skills to tell, returning from that height:

"Most" in line 1 is adverbial with "receives" and barely suggests the
partitive genitive of *più della sua luce*. The verb "receives" connotes more
passivity than *prende*. In line 2, "was I" closely renders the past definite
fu'io, as "saw" does *vidi*, but vagueness begins with "as man nor knows /
nor skills to tell." First of all, this adds a good deal to the Italian by

making the subject generic. The implication that this is an experience of mankind in general befogs the precision of the singular (though indefinite) subject understood and the singular pronoun of the Italian. Second, by pressure of English idiom (we cannot say that one "knows to tell"), as by the line division here, the alternatives suggested are knowing on the one hand and having skill to tell on the other, which misrepresents the original.

Binyon:

> In that heaven which partakes most of His light
> I have been, and have beheld such things as who
> Comes down thence has no wit nor power to write;

"Partakes most of His light" renders the active force of the Italian verb and partitive expression. "I have been," the English perfect, though a looser rendering of fu'io, is not only allowable but suitable to the tone of the passage as expressing a more contemplative and less purely narrative time sense. There is concision in "comes down thence," and "has no wit nor power" not only renders the alternatives correctly but unfolds what is latent in the two Italian verbs.

> perché appressando sé al suo disire,
>   nostro intelletto si profonda tanto,
>   che dietro la memoria non può ire.   [1.7–9]

Sayers:

> For when our intellect is drawing close
> To its desire, its paths are so profound
> That memory cannot follow where it goes.

The first line and a half closely render the Italian, but the next clause expands the metaphor with an image, "paths," that raises two questions: first, why the plural? and second, why such a degree of concreteness as to make that question arise? In line 3, dietro ire is presumed to mean "follow," implying a relationship between intellect and memory that is only superficially plausible.

Binyon:

Such depth our understanding deepens to
   When it draws near unto its longing's home
   That memory cannot backward with it go.

Here line 1 subtly embodies equivalences to the quality of the Italian: a four-syllable word, "understanding," to match and even chime with the participle *appressando*, and alliteration on four "ds" to match the "s's" and "ds" of the original. In line 3 the Italian is interpreted more precisely than in the Sayers version; here it is not that memory cannot "follow" the intellect but that it cannot return with it, taking *dietro* to mean "back," or indeed "back again," rather than "behind."

Are such points as these mere niggling? Before us on the open page is the philosophical poem of Christendom. It was written, as Ezra Pound once said, to make people think. In every line it exemplifies that activity. The translator's first job is to render Dante's meaning exactly and with delicacy. His second but no less crucial job is to render what he can—and again, with delicacy—of the verbal and metrical form in which the poet did his thinking. It seems that in both respects, again and again, one translation surpasses the other—not a bad one, either—bearing out what Pound said in *Broletto* about Binyon's idiom. But let us continue.

Veramente quant'io del regno santo
   nella mia mente potei far tesoro,
   sarà ora materia del mio canto.   [1.10–12]

Sayers:

Yet now, of that blest realm whate'er is found
   Here in my mind still treasured and possessed
   Must set the strain for all my song to sound.

"Whate'er" in line 1 rarefies the solid *quanto*. The agent *io* and the past action of treasuring up are transposed to a present passive construction. In the monosyllabic line 3, there is insensitive alliteration on four "s's," and the businesslike *sarà ora matera* becomes a tired poeticality, "must set the strain."
Binyon:

> Nevertheless what of the blest kingdom
>   Could in my memory, for its treasure, stay
>   Shall now the matter of my song become.

The echo of the Latin *verumtamen* in *Veramente* has been perceived and carried into the rendering. *Quanto* is, curtly, "what," and is first the subject of a past action as in the Italian it was the object of one, then the subject of a future statement exactly, and in exactly the same terms, as in the Italian.

> O buono Apollo, al' ultimo lavoro
>   fammi del tuo valor sì fatto vaso,
>   come dimandi a dar l'amato alloro.

Sayers:

> Gracious Apollo! in this crowning test
>   Make me the conduit that thy power runs through!
>   Fit me to wear those bays thou lovest best!

Here several displacements have occurred, from *buono* to "gracious" for Apollo, from *ultimo lavoro* to something quite different, a "crowning test," and most interesting of all, from *vaso* to a "conduit" through which the god's power is conceived to run. For the covert and intricate alliterative pattern of the third Italian line (*me . . . man . . . ma . . .* and *di . . . di . . . da*) we have "bays . . . best." In this final phrase a small ambiguity appears: do we understand that bays in general are what the god loves best, or that there are certain ("those") bays that among all bays he loves best?
Binyon:

> For the last labour, good Apollo, I pray,
>   Make me so apt a vessel of thy power
>   As is required for gift of thy loved bay.

Here lines 1 and 2, without obscurity or difficulty, adhere to the vocabulary of the Italian, including "vessel" for *vaso*, not less felicitous for not narrowing the conception to an open channel or pipe. The last line lacks any such obvious alliteration as that of the Sayers version, but the closing consonants of "gift" are quietly echoed by those of "loved," and the vowel sound of "required" is echoed by "thy."

V

Though Binyon finished his *Paradiso* without benefit of Pound's criticism, he undoubtedly brought to bear on it what he had absorbed from Pound's notes on the other two *cantiche*. As to the *Inferno*, in recording Pound's marginal notations in 1934 he said he intended some day to bring out a revised edition, and this in fact became a serious undertaking. Using an extra set of clean page proofs of the poem, he went through it canto by canto, penning in revisions of lines or passages that either he or Pound had found improvable. It is uncertain when most of this work was done; whether he did indeed wait until he had finished the *Paradiso* before returning to the "black air," as Pound suggested, or whether he began at once in 1934 and gave occasional hours to revision over the next eight or nine years. When he died he left among his papers a full set of page proofs of all thirty-four cantos, each bearing a number of revisions, in all more than 500, in almost all cases clear improvements.

The value of this concluding labor was clear to Binyon's widow, who typed out all the revisions and intended to have them incorporated in a new Macmillan printing. This has never taken place. The revisions remained among Binyon's papers until the late 1960s when Binyon's daughter, Nicolete (Mrs. Basil Gray), contrived to get them incorporated in the Viking Portable text, in a new edition dated 1969. The very first of these revisions may stand as representative of them all. Canto 1, line 1 of the *Inferno* in 1934:

Midway the journey of this life I was 'ware . . .

In the new edition:

Midway life's journey I was made aware . . .

The first version announced to the ear at once Binyon's system of elisions (journ'yof) and his deliberate allowance of a quota of archaism in style ('ware). Evidently to his later judgment, certainly influenced by Pound, these features were not enough to justify such a finicky line. He replaced it with what Pound called "straightness."

NOTES

1. Ezra Pound, "Hell," *Literary Essays of Ezra Pound*, ed. with an introduction by T. S. Eliot (London: Faber and Faber, 1954), p. 201.

2. Ezra Pound, *The Letters of Ezra Pound*, ed. D. D. Paige (New York: Harcourt, Brace & World, 1950), p. 251.

3. This and other letters of Laurence Binyon are quoted by kind permission of Nicolete Gray and The British Society of Authors. I am very grateful to Mrs. Gray for her consideration in placing these and other papers of her father at my disposal.

4. Quoted from letters in the possession of Nicolete Gray. For permission to use these letters I am grateful to the Literary Executors of Ezra Pound.

5. From a letter in the possession of Nicolete Gray.

6. Ezra Pound, *The Letters of Ezra Pound*, p. 310.

7. Ezra Pound, "Binyon," *Broletto* (Periodico della Citta di Como) 3 (October 1938): 14. For the opportunity of consulting this periodical and copying portions of Pound's article, I am indebted to the kindness of Professor Louis Martz, in 1975 director of the Beinecke Rare Book Library of Yale University.

8. F. T. Prince, *The Italian Element in Milton's Verse* (Oxford, 1954), rev. 1962.